Chuckler
is Alra
fixeD.
& Kristine for the
is Along
Ride of her life

Divorceless relationships

Wishing you
every happiness.
Mariah

Divorceless relationships

By Gary M. Douglas

and

Dr. Dain Heer

ACCESS/
CONSCIOUSNESS®
PUBLISHING

Divorceless relationships

Copyright © 2013 by Gary M. Douglas and Dr. Dain Heer

ISBN: 978-1-939261-04-5

Front Cover Design: Katarina Wallentin

Front Cover Design: Donielle Carter

Interior Design: Tori Burton

Published by Access Consciousness Publishing, LLC

www.accessconsciousnesspublishing.com

Printed in the United States of America
International printing in the U.K. and Australia
Second Edition

First Edition, copyright © 2011 by Gary M. Douglas, published by
Big Country Publishing, LLC

Contents

Foreword by Gary Douglas

Dain Heer and I have helped thousands of people with their relationships using the information you will find in this book. Our idea of relationship is that it should be something that expands your life, not something that contracts it. A relationship is not something you do as a substitute for having a life.

We have done a lot of research and we have gone to pretty much every church, cult and religion you could get involved in and neither one of us have found anything that gives you more freedom in this area than the tools of Access Consciousness. They offer more freedom, more choice and more possibilities than anything else we have tried.

Approximately 90% of the people we have worked with using these tools have had their relationship change into something better than what they had. They are able to begin generating the kind of relationship that actually works for both of them. The other 10% say, "You know what? This relationship isn't working. Neither of us really wants to be here. Let's get a divorce." And when they get a divorce they both get happier and everything works better in both of their lives. I am not saying the tools of Access are the answer, but I keep doing Access Consciousness because it works.

So, what do I know about the area of relationships that other people on the planet don't know? What makes me an authority?

Well, I had two marriages and both of them ended. Part of the reason they ended was that I was a romantic and I thought that if you loved somebody enough, everything would turn out fine. So whenever something about me was unacceptable to the person I was with, I would divorce that part of me in order to make the relationship work for them. And I began to realize that I not only did that in my marriages, I did it in all areas of my life as well.

For instance, I divorced certain parts of myself to talk to my family. My sister is a wonderful lady who has strong political views that are very intense, and I didn't always agree with everything she said. I used to try to share my point of view and then I discovered my point of view was not required or desired, so I kept my opinion to myself most of the time. Finally I got to the point where I realized I was divorcing parts of me by keeping quiet and trying not to step on her toes. I no longer do that.

We divorce ourselves in subtle ways. We tone down what we want to say or we say nothing at all. Or we say things in order to get somebody to agree with us. Most people will divorce themselves rather than ensnare themselves in a discussion that might result in a disagreement.

What if you were willing to always be you and state your point of view without trying to see the rightness or the wrongness of anyone's point of view, including yours? You would be able to say, "Okay, you know what? I may not agree with this, but are they wrong? No. Am I wrong? No. It's just a point of view." Would that eliminate some trauma and drama from your world?

Whenever you divorce any part of you and whenever you doubt that your own point of view has any value, you devalue you and make it as though you are nothing. That is not acknowledging you nor is it seeing the value of you.

What if you were to start to see the value of you in every relation-ship you have?

Whenever we go to the wrongness of us and judge ourselves, we are deciding that we have no value. What if the value of you was greater than you were able to see?

I invite you to use the information and the tools in this book to discover how not to feel compelled to divorce yourself in order to create a relationship with anybody. I encourage you to discover how to create divorceless relationships.

Are you ready to go on a journey to a whole different reality?

Chapter One

WHAT IS RELATIONSHIIP REALLY?

Relationship is defined as the distance between two objects. In other words, if you and I are in relationship, there has to be a separation between us—and we define our relationship by how close or far away we are from each other. When we create a relationship, we end up creating a separation from ourselves in an attempt to be close to somebody else. This is called monogamy. *Monogamy* by definition is a relationship with one and no other. The problem with this is that we tend to create relationship in such a way that we are the one who gets cut out because we always look to make the other person happy.

What happens for most people is this: They see each other and they are totally being themselves and there is an awareness of who the other amazing person is. This usually lasts about ten seconds.

Then each of you starts to cut off the parts and pieces of you that you think are going to be judged as not acceptable in the relationship—and then you are not being you anymore.

As you divorce parts of you to fit into the definition of the relationship you believe you desire, you create a divorce between you and the person you are with. They end up saying, "You are not the person I thought you were" and that is usually true, because you have divorced so much of yourself to try to make the relationship work.

Are you in an intimate relationship with someone? Ask yourself, "How many things am I willing to cut out of my life in order to be with that person?" Is it everything or nothing? Most of us spend a lot of time divorcing parts and pieces of us in order to care for someone else, and we give up caring for ourselves in the process. For example, you like to go jogging but instead of jogging, you spend that time with your partner as a way to show them you really care. "I love you so much that I would give up this thing that is valuable to me so I can be with you." This is one of the ways you divorce you to create an intimate relationship.

We want to give up these parts of us because we believe that will keep us from losing the other person, but in so doing, we lose the other person anyway. When you give up any part of yourself, you give up what was so attractive about you to that other person and pretty soon the other person doesn't want to be with you anymore.

Divorceless Relationship

A divorceless relationship is one where you don't have to divorce any part of you. Your relationships involve every aspect of life, so the tools for divorceless relationship apply to every aspect of your life, not just your partner or your family and friends. How is your relationship with money? How is your relationship with your business? Did you know you have a relationship with the things you own? How is your relationship with your garden, your car, and your house? What about your relationship with your body?

Dain is someone who thought he did relationship really well. He was the guy that a woman would definitely want to be in a relationship with because he would cut off his arms and legs to be in relationship with her.

For him, relationship was like when a friend drove up in a little Mini Cooper, honked the horn and said, "Hey, do you want to go on a ride?"

Dain would say, "I would totally love to go with you. That sounds like so much fun and maybe I'll even get sex out of it! Let me climb into the car." So he starts to get into the car but he can't put his feet in and he realizes his legs are too long for the Mini. He thinks, "Well, this is never going to work. I'll have to cut my legs off!" He cuts off his legs and climbs into the car but when he tries to shut the door he realizes his arms are too big. So he cuts them off too, so he can fit into the Mini and he can go on the ride. This is what most of us do in relationships.

We cut off our arms and legs to be with somebody and then wonder why we don't get around so well. Did that person ask you to cut off your arms and your legs? No. Did you ever think of saying, "Hey, I know you think a Mini is great, but it is not going to work for me. How about if we travel in a limousine? What if we both actually become more instead of having to go down a road that requires both of us to become less?"

This is the idea of what divorceless relationship is all about. It is the place where everyone and everything you are in a relationship with can become greater as a result of the relationship.

As you consider the places where you divorce yourself, we invite you to look from a different place and ask, "What am I really choosing here and what could I choose?" It is not that we want to give you the answer. We are not saying that if you do it our way, it is going to work. We just want you to see that there may be another possibility here that you have never considered. All we want to do for anybody is open those doors.

Chapter Two

FUNCTIONING AT ONLY
10% OF YOU

What percentage of you do you actually allow to show up in the world? More than 1% or less than 1%? If you have been even vaguely successful in life by functioning at less than 1% of you, can you imagine what you might be if you showed up as more than 1%? Where is the rest of you? Have you hidden it where you can't find it?

Do you ever say "part of me feels like…" or "part of me thinks…"? Do you realize you have divided you into parts and pieces so that you never have a whole you? How much of you have you divided into parts? How many pieces have you divided you into? More than 10,000 or less than 10,000? Probably more!

If you were a whole pie and you divided yourself into 10,000 pieces, how big a slice would you be? Not very big! Using these tools, you will start to get more and more of you back. It will not happen all at once, so don't look for that. Realize that if you get even five pieces of you back, that is 500% more of you than existed before!

Are you ready to change the entirety of your life and your world and your reality and everything you ever thought was true? You are on your way.

In order to make yourself feel like everyone else, you have to make sure to use not an ounce more than 10% out of the 1000% you actually have available. So 990% of you is what you have to cut off.

You keep to only 10% of your potency in order to not be hideously successful and not have way more money than you could ever spend, way more joy, way more fun, better relationships, way less trauma and drama and a lot more ease. What would it be like if you gave up your life of misery in favor of a life of fun, joy, happiness, possibilities, choices, questions and contribution? Of course, you don't want that. You want to be like other people, right?

What you are saying is, "I want to be as unhappy as everybody else because that way I know I totally fit in." This is what you have to do to function in contextual reality, which is all about where you fit, how you benefit, how you win and how you avoid losing.

The 10% Solution to Life

You were probably raised to believe your job in life was to get married, have 2.5 children and live happily ever after like everybody else. That is the 10% solution to life. Most women are taught that they are supposed to want to have a relationship and kids—but what about the women who are more into conquering the world than having home and hearth? How about the men who are more interested in home and hearth than conquering the world?

We are all programmed from the time we are little to believe that the 10% solution is what we are supposed to do. All the movies and television programs you see, all the songs and stories you hear are about getting married and living happily ever after. How many people do you know that got married and actually lived happily ever after?

In order to fit into this program, you will never allow yourself to use more than 10% of you. Occasionally you may have the brilliant day where you allow 12% to show up, and then miracles happen. How often do you have a 12% day and then say, "I'd better drop down to 8% tomorrow so I can even things out and still fit in?" How much energy does it take for you to be only 10% of you?

If you functioned at 12% you would be considered a brilliant person in this reality. At 15% you would be considered an extraordinary person. Oprah is probably at about 18% and Richard Branson, the phenomenal British entrepreneur, is at about 20%. What if you stepped beyond that? What could you be? What could you create?

Being the 990%

Dain went and bought a bicycle the other day so he could ride up and down the hills around our house at six in the morning. Everybody else says, "Oh I hate those hills. Can we go on a flat area please? Nice gentle slopes are okay, but hills, no!" Dain says, "Yay! Hills!" He rides in the hills and says, "Wow, that was fun!" Most people say, "You are sick!" But Dain is willing to be "sick" because it feels more like the 990% to him. When you are willing to live the 990%, you are willing to do what others are not willing to do. It's fun for you.

You can be totally calm in the sea of adversity around you and not have a point of view about it. You can be you in the middle of the sea and say, "Wow, it is so cool being me right now. I don't have to worry about solving any of this for anybody. I don't have to worry about trying to change it for anybody in order for me to be me."

Choosing to be the 990% of you is not about making yourself superior to others. It is about the awareness of who you truly are.

Let's say you have a BMW and you also have a Vespa. Can the Vespa go faster than the BMW or is the BMW faster than the Vespa? The BMW is inherently faster but it doesn't make itself wrong for being faster. It just is. The problem occurs if you are a BMW and you are trying to make yourself into a Vespa!

Making you less does not make others more. Dain has this weird talent and ability to be able to morph his body in a heartbeat. He will go out for a run, and without working out with weights, he will come back with bigger arms and a bigger chest. But when he gets around somebody who feels bad about their body, he can shrink his body so he's four inches shorter than they are. Why does he do that? Because the other guy feels bad about himself, and Dain doesn't want him to feel bad. How well does that actually work? Have you ever tried to do this? It doesn't ever work, but you keep doing it!

As a kid at school, did you put things off and wait to the last minute, because you didn't want to take unfair advantage? You always knew you could get an A if you studied just a little bit harder, but instead you would wait until the eleventh hour every time. Did you believe that by studying a little more that you were taking advantage? The thing is, you are advantaged; don't assume you are anything less.

Making you less does not make the other person like himself more! He's never going to be anything more than what he has decided he is. The only thing that ever actually works is you being willing to be you as the 990% and to be all of that. Then maybe there's a possibility that someone will look at you and say, "You know what, if he or she can be that, then maybe so can I." The only possibility you have of changing someone else's feeling bad about who they are is by being an invitation to something greater.

So how do you get to being the 990%? That's what the tools in this book will show you.

Chapter Three

WHAT WOULD AN
INFINITE BEING DO?

Before we begin to show you how the tools of Access Consciousness work, there is something that has to be established. Are you aware that you are an infinite being?

Be willing to have this awareness. You are not just your body; your body isn't what you are.

Exercise: *Close your eyes (after you read this part, of course!). Now feel out with your awareness and find the outside edges of you. Not your body, the edges of YOU. Can you? Or everywhere you look, are you there? Yes, everywhere you look, there you are!*

Okay. Open your eyes. The space that you were aware of when you were feeling out with your awareness—that space that is everywhere and infinite—is YOU. You are an infinite being.

So are you capable of being inside something as small as your body? Or does your body fit inside of you?

Your body is inside of you; you are not inside your body.

You cannot define an infinite being because as soon as you define it, it is no longer infinite. People say, "Well, if I am an infinite being, I should have a joyous, happy life. So why is my life screwed up? If I am an infinite being, how is it that I can't afford rent? If I am an infinite being, how is it that I am unhappy most of the time?" Well, as you go through this book, you are going to find out why. You are going to find a lot of ways to unlock the joy, bliss and ecstasy that is infinite being.

All you need to know right now is that if you're not choosing joy, bliss and ecstasy, there is a different option available. Wouldn't it be nice if trauma and drama seemed irrelevant? Imagine someone saying, "Come on, you need to get into a fight with me!" And your viewpoint would be "Why would I spend that much energy? Why would I spend the energy it takes to get depressed when I could just enjoy my day?" Are you aware that it takes energy to get depressed? You have to use a lot of energy to get depressed. That is weird, isn't it? It feels like you have no energy when you are doing depression. Why is that? Because you are using it all to be depressed!

If you were truly being the infinite being you are, you and everything in your life would be intense and expansive. Remember when you were a kid. Was every day way too short and did it have too much in it? Have you ever noticed that kids have fun all the time? When you are choosing infinite beingness, you can have fun all the time, just like a kid.

In this contextual reality true joy, bliss and ecstasy may seem impossible but somewhere in your world, you know it is supposed to be different, don't you? You must—or you wouldn't be reading this book.

Tool: Would an Infinite Being Choose This?

This is the number one tool. Ask the question **"Would an infinite being choose this?"** If an infinite being wouldn't choose it, then why would you?

The question is designed to get you to look at where you are functioning from. Yes, you are an infinite being but you are not functioning as an infinite being. You function as a finite being within the 10%.

You don't have to live in a constant state of destruction of you. There is a different choice. You have to be willing to pay attention to what you say and what you think at every moment. Every time you say, "I feel I can't…" or "This is so hard for me…" ask yourself, **"Would an infinite being choose this?"**

If an infinite being wouldn't choose it, then perhaps you may wish to choose differently!

The only reason you are choosing something that an infinite being wouldn't choose is to make yourself finite and to create a disaster in your life. You didn't know you liked creating disaster, did you? Literally, you are creating the disasters in your life. You keep assuming "I wouldn't create this if I had another choice!" Is that really true?

The truth is that you are the creator of everything in your life. This is very good news because if you created it, you can uncreate and change it too!

Asking **"Would an infinite being choose this?"** invites you to look at what is going on for you and brings you the awareness of what you can be or do that will change it. When you claim, own and acknowledge your creations without judgment, you bring back all the parts and pieces of you that you have divorced and you acknowledge your infinite perceiving, knowing, being and receiving.

Perceiving, Knowing, Being and Receiving

Knowing, perceiving, being and receiving are what you are as an infinite being. Thoughts, feelings, emotions, sex or no sex are the lower harmonic of those things. They keep you in contextual reality and the 10%.

Total consciousness is our innate being. If we destroy everything that doesn't allow that to show up, it will manifest as more awareness. You as the infinite being will always show up as more of the infinite being you are. This is the reason for using the tools and for doing the clearings you will find in this book.

Thoughts and Knowing

Have you ever tried to think yourself out of a problem? Does it ever really work? Or do you just tie yourself into knots? You tie yourself into knots because *thinking* requires effort and contraction. If you *knew,* you wouldn't have to think things through. All you would have to do is tap into the infinite knowledge that's available to us all. Have you ever had moments where you just knew something? What's faster? Thinking or knowing?

If you are thinking you are stinking. Your mind can only define the limitations of what you already know and have. It doesn't open doors to the world of possibilities; it only defines what you cannot be, do, have, create or generate. It will never show you what is possible in life. Your mind is a terrible thing; waste it.

Feeling and Perceiving

Perception is like the wind. It moves and changes. Perception is about being aware of energies; perception is fleeting. Perception gives you awareness of what you can choose and how that will change things energetically. If you are willing to have infinite perception, then you have infinite choice. Perception is large. It's like a giant field where wheat is growing. The wind blows the wheat and you can see it undulating into different forms as the wind strikes it. The more perception you have, the greater your picture of what's occurring in the world.

We have the capacity to perceive the whole world the way we perceive the wheat field, but instead we try to *feel* some way about it so we can define it, which we think will enable us to control it and keep it in a context that makes sense to us. When you try to twist your awareness into feeling, you are trying to make it solid so that you can do something with it.

Most feelings and emotions are about a negative point of view, not about a positive thing. They seldom contribute to expanding your awareness or your reality. That's because in order to create feeling, we must cut off our awareness.

Emotions and Being

Thoughts, feelings, emotions, sex or no-sex are the lower harmonics of being, perceiving, knowing and receiving. They are the limited version of these. If you are functioning as an infinite being, then you have an infinite capacity to experience everything and you don't have to define it, confine it and put it into a place where it makes sense according to someone else's point of view. You are simply aware that you have these things. Most people start out as little kids with giant perceptions of things and they're told, "That is not so." They are trained to put things in context with feelings.

As a child, I would perceive something and mention it to my mother.

She would say, "Oh, that person is feeling sad."

What I felt was far greater than sadness. It was far more than anything that had been perceived as sadness. But when she said it had to be defined as sadness, I thought, "I must be wrong. I must not understand this. I must have a misconception," and I began to cut off my awareness of all the other things that were going on so I could define my perceptions according to my mother's description. I put my perception into the slot she had defined it as. We tend to do this with the people we are close to.

People say things like, "Oh, I am so hurt by what you said!"

Are they really hurt? Or is that a way of proving that they are *being* something? They define themselves as the emotion. They are being highly emotional. They use the trauma and the drama of things to prove that they are actually being something. They think that if they are hurt, upset, angry or whatever, that's who they are. No. That's just a fragment of who and what they are.

In a similar way, some people choose bad relationships to prove that they don't deserve to be loved. Some people choose to be hungry in order to prove they don't deserve nurturing, caring and sex. Some choose to be a demon bitch or a bastard from hell to prove they don't deserve nice people in their life. When you are functioning from true being and awareness, you don't have to try to prove things with your emotions.

18

Sex/No Sex and Receiving

We talk about "no sex" because it is the 10% reality of no receiving. Receiving in this sense is not a completion; it doesn't mean we get something. True receiving occurs as simultaneous gifting and receiving. When you can receive everything, then you can expand your life exponentially every day!

Have you ever awakened on a spring morning and the birds were singing and the sun was shining and you just felt so alive? When you feel that alive, you are willing to receive everything. Let's say you are driving on one of those days and somebody cuts you off and you respond with, "Okay, yeah, have a good time. See you later." You feel great and you are willing to "receive" that interaction without becoming the effect of it. Then there are those days when you wake up and you hit the snooze alarm and by the tenth snooze you are in such a bad mood you don't want to get up at all. That is the no sex energy, the place of no receiving.

The energy of sex is actually the receiving energy of your body. The energy of sex is when you are feeling good, looking good and strutting your stuff. That is sex. No sex is the opposite when you are saying, "Stay away, I don't want anything to do with anybody." You are not open for receiving; you literally put up the walls so you don't receive anything. That is that no sex position.

This allows you to ask, "Wait a minute, am I choosing the 10% of no sex or am I choosing the 990% of infinite receiving that I actually could choose?"

People think receiving is getting money or getting a relationship or getting something. No, receiving is living joyfully. When you live joyfully, you can receive anything, and therefore everything you ask for comes to you. When you get this, you can change everything and have a totally different life.

What Are You Willing to Receive?

How do you know when you are not willing to receive something? When you are not allowing it to be in your life.

Exercise: *Go to a store and look at all the things you would not buy. Anything you will not buy is something you will not receive from. This exercise will show you all the places where you are creating limitations in your life. Ask yourself, "Am I willing to have this? Or am I just pretending I am willing to have this?" Wherever you have decided "I will not buy this" is a place you cannot receive. This is the easiest way to find out what you will not receive in life.*

Everything you aren't willing to buy is an indication of what you are choosing to eliminate from your life. That doesn't mean you have to buy it, but you have to be willing to receive the energy of it.

A lady we work with did this exercise and she realized that she couldn't even see some of the things that were in the store because she was unwilling to receive them in her life. She said, "Gary told me to do this exercise, so I went to a store I have gone into at least fifty times. I would buy almost anything in this store because I love jewels, but because I was doing the exercise, I started to look at what I would not buy there. Although I had thought I would probably choose to buy everything they had, I found lots of things that I wouldn't buy. And I saw things in the store I didn't even know they sold, which was very interesting."

Going to a shop is a way you can start opening doors to the awareness of what you are not willing to have. When you start looking at what you wouldn't buy, you are looking for the things you have decided you don't like. If you don't like something, you will not receive the energy of it in your life. This exercise brings your attention to all the places you say, "I don't like that, I won't receive that, I am never going to do that or I am never going to have that."

You should be able to notice everything. Every time you decide "I wouldn't have that in my life," you cut off a level of your awareness. When there isn't anything you are not willing to have in your life, you can walk into a room and feel the energy of everything around you. You will notice when something has been added or when something isn't there, because energetically you are willing to have all of those things in your life.

What you want to get from this exercise is the willingness to look at things and ask, "Okay, what if I had that in my life? What would change in my life if I was willing to have this? If I was willing to have this in my life, what would my life be like?" Whenever you decide "I will not have that in my life" there is a thing you will not receive from. If you become willing to have that, then you are willing to receive a different kind of energy.

For example, I like horses, but years ago I rode some Appaloosas, which have spots on their rump, and they were so stupid and stubborn that they were not fun to ride. I decided, "I don't like Appaloosas." I would not receive them as anything except "stubborn and stupid." Then I came across a different kind of horse that also had spots on its rump, but it wasn't an Appaloosa. A horse that had spots and that wasn't stubborn and stupid did not compute in my world. All I could see was spotted rump, which meant Appaloosa, which meant stupid and stubborn.

Non-contextual reality is about possibilities, choice, question and contribution. If you have decided in the contextual universe that there's a loss in riding Appaloosas or that you don't win if you ride

Appaloosas, or that riding Appaloosas doesn't fit you or there's no benefit to riding Appaloosas, then you cannot allow anyone who's willing to ride Appaloosas to contribute to your life.

That doesn't mean to say you have to ride Appaloosas. It becomes a choice. You just have to recognize that by the points of view you take, you eliminate what can contribute to your life. The question here is: Would you be willing to let anyone or anything contribute to your life?

Infinite Beings Don't Have Lessons to Learn

Are you functioning from the point of view that you have lessons to learn? What if there was nothing to learn from anything?

You are an infinite being. You have had thousands of lifetimes, actually more like millions of lifetimes, so do you think there is anything you haven't been or done? No. Would you really have a lesson to learn? No. You can be less conscious, which is where you think you get lessons to learn—or you can be more conscious and then you know you have nothing to learn.

You can access new awarenesses, but that is not about lessons, it is about accessing more consciousness. How much of the consciousness you could have are you refusing by believing you have to learn lessons? Are you willing to access more consciousness in your life?

When you realize that you, the infinite being, can choose anything, you can choose something that is greater and more dynamic and more fun than what everybody else is choosing.

You are the only power source you can't totally overcome. You have enough power to stop you—but nobody else does. Nobody else can stop you from doing anything. You, however, will stop you all the time.

How do you do that? With every judgment you make of you. "How do I hate me, let me count the ways." You are really good at that.

Chapter Four

WHAT AM I DOING WRONG?

Innate wrongness is what you usually feel as a child. You know you are wrong and that somehow it is wrong to be everything you are. What is going on here? You are getting projection from your parents about what wrong means to them. They may have looked at you and thought, "Well, that girl is trouble looking for a place to happen" and the energy you get is the wrongness of you.

Here is an example from Dain's life: Dain's mother is gay and Dain's whole family was afraid Dain would also be gay, which was wrong as far as they were concerned. So what was constantly projected at him? Their desire for him to be something that would never equal gay. Does that make him have to fit in a box that makes their world work? Yes. Where is Dain's choice in that?

Dain's father, his mother, his grandmother, and his whole family took the point of view that "He's definitely not going to be gay; he may be sexual but he's not going to be gay." So he was allowed to be sexual, but he was not allowed to have choice. He had to put out sexual energy towards every woman that he saw.

When someone projects that kind of intensity of point of view on you, you will try to fit into their world instead of having your own. This is not about being gay or straight; this is about how you make yourself wrong because wherever choice has been eliminated from your world based on the box your family tried to put you into (which had nothing to do with you) you come up with you being the wrongness of all things.

Tool: Who Does This Belong To?

Here is a key piece of information: Ninety eight percent of your thoughts, feelings and emotions do not belong to you. You are incredibly psychic. You can pick up all the depression, upset and other feelings of the people around you and you assume they are yours. They are not. How can you choose *your* life when the thoughts, feelings and emotions you are having are not actually yours in the first place? You can't. You try to live your life based on all the stuff you pick up from other people, but the reality is that what you pick up has nothing to do with you.

For instance, how many of the judgments you have are actually yours in the first place?

Dain credits this tool with saving his life. He says, "Ten years ago I was going to kill myself. I had even planned the date for it and then I had a session of Bars* and it changed everything. During the Bars session, Shannon (my facilitator) told me, "Ninety-eight percent of your thoughts, feelings and emotions don't belong to you." I said, "Yeah, right." She even wrote the tool **"Who does this belong to?"** on a piece of paper for me. Usually in the mornings, after my fiancée left for work, I would cry because I didn't know how I was going to make my life work. I had tried so many things and I was so frustrated. One morning I was lying there crying and I pulled out this little paper and read, "Who does this belong to?" Instantaneously the tears and the frustration went away. I was pissed and elated at the same time. Pissed because somebody should have told me this when I was born! Then I wouldn't have had to go through all the insanity and depression and hating myself and wanting to kill myself! Elated because it literally vanished! I was like, "What the fuck just happened?" That's when I really got it—98% of your thoughts, feelings and emotions don't belong to you. I committed to doing the three day exercise that very day and I have never looked back."

Three Day Exercise: *Ask, **"Who does this belong to?"** for every thought, feeling and emotion you have for three days. You don't need to get an answer; you just need to ask the question. If the energy lightens up when you ask the question, then it is not yours. Return it to sender. At the end of three days you walk around like you are a walking, talking meditation. You will have no thoughts in your head at all.*

Asking the question **"Who does this belong to?"** will alert you to when you are functioning from something that is not really your point of view. You don't need to identify whether it is a thought, a feeling or an emotion. Anything that is not truly you will feel like a contraction, because all thoughts, feelings and emotions are a contraction of being. If it's easier, you can recall a time when you were in a space of total peace and joy and then when you experience anything that doesn't feel like that, ask, **"Who does this belong to?"**

26

The way this exercise works is that on the first day you will manage to do about thirty minutes before you feel exhausted, and then about two hours later you will remember you are supposed to be doing it and start again. You will get forty minutes that time and then you will say, "Whoa, that's just way too much work! I had no idea there were so many thoughts, feelings and emotions coming at me all the time that I was unaware of." And then a couple of hours later you will remember again and you will do fifty minutes. That's the first day. You will go to sleep early that night because you are exhausted from having paid attention to all the things you received.

The second day when you perceive a thought, emotion or feeling, you ask, **"Who does this belong to?"** it just disappears. You will end up doing it for maybe an hour and a half and then you will forget. You will go back to it again for maybe two hours and that's the end of that day. The next day you will get up and start to do it and somewhere around the middle of the third day all of a sudden it gets quiet in your head. It feels like space.

Many people will not do this exercise because they are unwilling to allow this to occur. Why? Because when you do this, you become way more aware of other people's universes and their insanities and you may feel like it will drive you crazy. The truth is that as you return things to sender, you have a greater sense of space and it gets a lot easier to perceive what's going on with other people without being the effect of it.

Your ability to be aware cannot be stopped. You can try to alter your awareness or refuse it, but that doesn't really work. Be willing to recognize your awareness—and then choose to use it instead of refusing it.

Awareness comes a little at a time. You don't just instantly step into total awareness. You will have realizations like, "Wow, this wasn't mine in the first place" and then you begin to notice other places where you are taking on things that aren't yours.

Being Wrong in Relationship

How does being wrong show up in your relationships? Say your partner feels something is wrong with his or her life. You will automatically assume you are wrong. There is no other choice—because anything that has to do with "wrong" has to be about you.

Once you have decided you are wrong, you will either try to fix the situation or you will think that there is something that you need to turn off. You will ask, "What part of me do I have to shut off in order to not have this wrongness?" We tend to turn off a huge amount of us in the process of trying to figure out how to fix us. Then you begin to notice that when the thing that you have concluded is wrong in you is turned off, the "wrongness" energy isn't projected at you.

If the projection that you are interpreting as wrongness is still there, you turn something else off, and then something else, until finally you get the "right" thing and you say, "Oh, when I turn this off, that isn't projected at me so I'm going to keep it turned off." The only trouble is everything else you have turned off is shut down as well, because you don't remember having turned it off anymore.

Now you have separated yourself into parts and pieces that are okay and not okay. This is the way you keep yourself separate from you. You spend your time trying to keep you in a confined place that is just barely acceptable to you. You decide this place is "okay." Isn't it sad that what is most valuable to us is to be okay? Not fabulous, amazing, wonderful or phenomenal—just okay.

Rather than looking at you and seeing the value of you, you see the judgeable offense you think you are. What judgeable offense have you defined yourself as in order to prove you don't deserve a better life?

A judgeable offense is the perception that life should be a certain way, but you want to live it this other way. You define yourself as a judgeable offense when you think, "I really should be perfect— and I am not. I should be perfect, I should be greater, I should be, I should be, I should be." Every "should" is a judgeable offense.

You always assume you should be better than what you are. What if you were not as fucked up as you think you are? Would you consider the possibility that you are already greater than you believe you are?

Chapter Five

WHAT PART DOES JUDGMENT PLAY?

Have you ever noticed that nobody judges you as harshly as you do? You think that if you judge yourself harshly enough, eventually you will find the good parts of you. Were you taught that to judge yourself was the way to find you? What if you didn't have to judge anything? What if you found out you actually like you? What if everything was a choice?

Remember that in relationship there is a distance between you and someone else. You create less distance between you and the people you are close to and *more* distance between you and the people you don't feel close to. We use judgment to create that distance. Every judgment you create requires a greater distance from the person you are judging, so every time you do any judgment, it results in distance. The problem with this is that the person you judge the most is you; so you are creating a greater and greater distance of you away from you.

What part of you have you decided is not acceptable? Is it so unacceptable that you have hidden it? And have you hidden it so well that you have lost track of where it is? This is what we do. We put that unacceptable part of us out of existence and this creates the separation of you from you. Soon you have little to no relationship with yourself at all.

Whenever you make a judgment about anything, you eliminate your capacity to perceive anything that does not match it. As soon as you do a judgment, you come to a conclusion, and once you do that, you cannot see that another choice is available.

Let's say you are having a conversation with someone, and you realize that they are not getting what you are saying. You may respond to this by making yourself wrong for not being believed. Or you may try to make them wrong for not believing you. Either of these decisions puts you into judgment.

Most people use judgment to create safety and predictability in their lives. They figure if they judge hard enough they will know who to have in their lives and who not to have in their lives; they will know who will hurt them and who won't hurt them. The thing is they have already judged that somebody *will* hurt them; they have not asked, "Will this person hurt me? Yes or no?"

This is where relationships get into trouble, because no one asks questions. People just make assumptions and judgments about what is going to occur.

The Power of Allowance

We would like to introduce you to the concept of allowance, where everything is included and nothing is judged. When you are in allowance, you allow things to be as they are until they show up differently. Allowance is being willing to see what is and have no point of view about it. You don't feel that something *has* to change; it's okay if it changes and it's okay if it doesn't change. When you are in allowance, you are willing to be aware. Ultimate freedom lies in the awareness that awareness is just awareness. It is not right or wrong or good or bad. It is just awareness.

Allowance is not acceptance. Acceptance is alignment and agreement (the positive view) or resistance and reaction (the negative view). With acceptance, you accept that "this is the way it is" and there is nothing you can do about it. Or you see something as right, good, perfect and correct. With resistance and reaction, you accept that things are bad, wrong, mean and terrible. It's easy to see how acceptance is alignment and agreement, but you may ask, "How can acceptance also be resistance and reaction?" This is how it works: In order to be in resistance and reaction, you have to align with the other person's point of view to some extent, and you then resist and react to it. Either way—whether you align and agree or resist and react, you take a point of view that locks you up.

Allowance is knowing that everything anyone else might say or do is just an interesting point of view. It has no relationship to you. You don't have to align and agree with someone else's point of view or resist and react to it, nor do they have to do this with your points of view.

Allowance does not mean disregarding your point of view. In this reality, people commonly believe that allowance means that you must disregard your own point of view and decide that everything is okay just the way it is. Sometimes people think you are not in allowance if you ask for things to change to suit you or that you should always see the positive in everyone and trust in the greater good. This definition of allowance requires you to become a doormat. It encourages you to make other people's reality more valuable than your awareness. It is a definition that sounds true—but it is really a logical lie, and it sticks you in polarity.

Allowance is not about tolerance or patience. Tolerance is "putting up with." It is actually resistance and reaction to a situation or a person. Tolerance is what you do when you are pissed off and frustrated and you let the other person continue to do what they are doing even though you are not at all happy about them doing it.

If you tolerate someone abusing you, you are at the mercy of their abuse and unable to direct what happens next. If you are tolerant, you are agreeing to suffer in silence. To be in allowance is to acknowledge their choice and be willing to choose for you. You can say, "I'm sorry, this doesn't work for me. Don't do this when I'm with you. Do it somewhere else please." And walk away.

Patience is waiting for someone or something to change and being in judgment of it not changing the whole time. You are putting your life on hold until something changes. There is no choice in patience. It requires judgment and being vested in the outcome. It puts the source for your choice outside of you so all you can do is wait. Patience is "I have to hold out."

My youngest son used to drink heavily, and he is obnoxious when he is drunk. I said, "You know what, Son, I hate you when you drink. You are the most obnoxious son of a bitch I have ever met in my life, and so this is the deal. Don't come to my house when you are drunk. Don't go out with me when you are drunk. You get obnoxious with the waitresses and do things that don't cut it for me. I am going to get up and leave the next time you do it; I don't want to be around you when you are drinking."

He said, "What about allowance, Dad? Where's your willingness to let me do whatever I want?"

I replied, "I am willing to let you do it; I am not killing you, am I? You can do whatever you want, just don't do it around me, because I will not put up with this shit. Your getting drunk doesn't work for me."

This is allowance, and it created a space where something could change for my son. He still drinks, but he has cut down on the amount and he doesn't drink to excess when he is around me. He's much more controlled with it. And he no longer drinks and drives with his two-year-old in the car.

You have to include *you* **in allowance.** Another key point about allowance is that you have to include you in it. Allowance for you means being willing to have allowance for exactly how you are without any judgment and without any necessity of changing you. What would it be like if you actually had allowance of you?

Allowance is "interesting point of view" without judgment. Judgment creates polarity and there is no freedom in polarity. There is only positive and negative, right and wrong or good and bad. Every time you create a judgment, nothing that doesn't match your judgment can come into your awareness. You have to let go of the judgment in order to have the freedom of you.

Other people's thoughts, feelings and emotions come at you and you are aware of them but they don't impact you. They go around you, and you are still you.

A lady wrote me an eight-page letter of judgments about how wrong I was. I asked her, "Do you want to handle this?"

She said, "No, I am just waiting for you to change."

I said, "Well, I hate to tell you, darling, but I am not going to change because you have judgments of me. I am willing to deal with your judgments of me so that we can have a closer relationship, but as long as you are standing over here judging me, how close can our relationship be?"

Unfortunately she was more interested in judging me than she was being close to me. I was more interested in being close than I was in her judgment. It is always just a choice.

Tool: It's Just an Interesting Point of View

What would it be like to have no point of view about anything? Not to insist that you are right or wrong or that you are good or bad or that you are black or white or anything else, but to see everything as just an interesting point of view. The truth is that everybody's point of view is just their point of view. There is no right nor wrong nor good nor bad; it is all just a point of view. What if you were willing to look at everything and go, "Wow, that is an interesting point of view?"

Look at nature. Think of a spring day when it is all calm and beautiful and suddenly there is a volcanic eruption that kills lots of people and animals and destroys the land. Does nature have a point of view about this? No, it just is. Have you ever wondered why being in nature feels so good? It's because nature has no point of view.

Here is a tool you can use that will give you huge amounts of freedom. We invite you to use it continuously for one full year. For every point of view you notice you have, say, **"Interesting point of view I have this point of view"** and let it go. At some point while doing this, you will suddenly get to the recognition that you really have no point of view about much of anything. Even the points of view that you keep hearing and perceiving from other people become just an interesting point of view. You no longer have the point of view that any of it belongs to you. You don't have to take a point of view and you never have to be right. The beauty of this is that once you never have to be right, you can just be correct.

When you judge you, are you in allowance of you? No. Would you be willing to notice when you are taking a point of view about yourself and say, **"Interesting point of view I have that point of view about me?"**

When you realize that everything is just an interesting point of view, all of a sudden you ask, "What would I like to choose here?" You are in a place where choice begins and rightness ends. When you are doing rightness, all choice ceases because you cannot have rightness and choice together.

To live as "interesting point of view" is being aware of your point of view and not aligning with or resisting another person's point of view.

You don't have to do anything about your awarenesses. You simply allow others to have their point of view, to do whatever they are doing, in whatever way they are doing it, without feeling the requirement to change you or them. You allow others to be everything they are without expecting anything of them. The problem is that people think that if they don't judge something as wrong, then they are condoning it or seeing it as right. Being in allowance frees you from the judgment trap.

Each time you take a point of view that is fixed, you are not living in the question and the curiosity; you are living in the answer. Every answer creates a system for judgment.

Living in the Question

For most of us, living above the 10% has always been our desire. It is what we have always looked for. Have you spent your entire life seeking something that would give you the awareness you were looking for through metaphysics, religion or anything else? Everybody would say, "This is the answer!" and you would go, "Okay, that looks like the answer, okay cool." Then you would

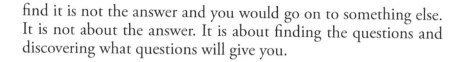

find it is not the answer and you would go on to something else. It is not about the answer. It is about finding the questions and discovering what questions will give you.

Tool: Live in the Question

Have you ever noticed that you keep choosing the same kind of relationship over and over again? One of the reasons you continue to do this is because you don't ask questions. You don't ask, "What do I really require or desire?" You don't consult your awareness and you continue to choose the same person in a different body over and over again. How do you change this? You live in the question.

Living in the question will take you out of looking for answers, which is what keeps you in contextual reality and the 10%. What is contextual reality? Contextual reality is the way the majority of the world functions. It is the way we have learned to figure out where we are and where we want to get to in life.

In contextual reality, you function from these four positions:

- How do I fit?
- How do I benefit?
- How can I win?
- How can I avoid losing?

You have to use a lot of energy figuring out your place in the context of things, and one of the things you use contextual reality for is to make yourself wrong. You judge you for being what is wrong in your relationships.

There is another way of living, which is different; it's non-contextual reality. We have all had times in our lives when magic and miracles occur and everything works easily. This is what non-contextual reality is about.

In non-contextual reality, you function from these four positions:

🌸 What are the possibilities here?

🌸 What questions can I ask to generate something different?

🌸 What choices do I have?

🌸 What contribution can I be and receive?

A non-contextual relationship is completely different because it does not require you to judge you or to cut off any part of you to make the relationship work. You can choose your relationship to be anything you would like it to be. If it's not working, you can ask, "What would have to change for this to work for me?" You are not asking, "What do I have to change about me?" You are asking for a different possibility, one that does not require you to divorce you from you.

Living in the question allows for more possibility. Many people assume a question requires an instantaneous answer so they look for it in the contextual universe. "Okay, if I ask the right question then I can win, I won't lose and I will benefit by the question that I ask." The majority of the world operates from the point of view that if they can somehow get it right, then everything in their life will work. Unfortunately it doesn't actually work that way. The target here is to get to the point where you see questions not as a completion, but as a possibility. You don't want to look for the right answer. You want to look for the right question. What question will create the most possibilities here?

Tool: Four Questions for Everything

✳ What is this?

✳ What do I do with it?

✳ Can I change it?

✳ How do I change it?

Sometimes you can't change it. Or if you can change it, you might not be able to change it right now. So ask, "When can I change it?" The key thing to remember is that if you get into a funk, ask questions. Whenever you feel stuck, it's time to ask a question. So many times when we're in a funk, we never think to ask one simple question **"What's it going to take to change this?"**

Chapter Six

YOU CAN TRUST THE ENERGY

Words have an energy to them. Every question we ask, every word we use, has an energy to it, and when we ask a question, that energy goes into action.

For example, how often do you say, "I want?" In modern dictionaries, the word want means to desire, but in dictionaries published prior to 1946, there are 26 definitions for *want* which mean to lack. To want is to lack or to be without. Every time you say, "I want," you are bringing in the energy of "I lack." When you say, "I want a relationship," you are saying, "I lack of a relationship." What are you going to get when you say, "I lack?" More lack.

We don't even realize we are using words like *want* incorrectly because we have been misinformed about what they mean. Try this just for the fun of it. See if this makes you feel lighter and more expanded or heavier and more contracted. Say out loud, "I don't want more money." Say it ten times.

"I don't want more money. I don't want more money. I don't want more money. I don't want more money. I don't want more money. I don't want more money. I don't want more money. I don't want more money. I don't want more money. I don't want more money."

Do you feel lighter or heavier? You feel lighter because you are saying, "I don't lack of more money," which means you are now willing to have more money in your life.

If you are not in a relationship and you would like to be, try this and see what happens: Say ten times "I don't want a relationship."

"I don't want a relationship. I don't want a relationship. I don't want a relationship. I don't want a relationship. I don't want a relationship. I don't want a relationship. I don't want a relationship. I don't want a relationship. I don't want a relationship. I don't want a relationship."

Notice how much better you feel when you say that, because you've been working like crazy to create a relationship with someone who doesn't want the relationship you want.

Language is energy, so when you use a word, it creates an energy. When you look at the definitions of what you are saying, you may often find that a word has a totally different energy than what you think you are saying. If you are overweight, you can say, "I don't want to be skinny anymore." Say it ten times in the morning and ten times in the evening, and see what happens to your body.

How Do I Know What Is True?

Truth and what is *true* are two different energies. *Truth* is a fixed point of view; it is an answer and usually a judgment. A truth is a solidity whereas *true* is a perception of what is in this moment. It can change. Everything must be malleable and movable or you are stuck. Whenever you take a fixed point of view about what is true, it has to become a lie in a very short period of time, because every fixed point of view is a limitation. That which is *a truth* becomes a fixed point of view, which stops the energy and leaves you stuck in it.

Tool: Does It Feel Light or Heavy?

It is characteristic of energy that when you ask the question **"Is this true?"** you will be able to perceive the energy of it. That which is a lie will always make you feel heavier and that which is true will always make you feel lighter.

Which one feels lighter to you? *True?* Or *truth?* If you're like most people, *true* feels lighter. So you ask, **"Is this true?"** If you ask and there's a lightness to it, you know that it is true. If you ask, "Is this a lie?" it will feel heavy until you acknowledge that it is a lie; and then it will feel light because it is true that it is a lie.

We encourage you to use this tool with everything you read in this book.

There is no logical explanation for how this works. It just does. Logic is the idea that everything can be explained. Can you explain why the sun shines? Can you really explain it, or do you take the scientific explanation and apply what they say as though it is true? Is science looking for what is true—or is it looking for the truth?

The explanations scientists came up with fifty years ago that were proven to be true scientifically at the time are considered hogwash today. What we consider scientific today will be seen as hogwash in another fifty years. So why are we buying science as truth now? What's the truth today will be a lie next week or next year or in the next ten seconds.

Tool: Is This a Truth With a Lie Attached?

Have you ever had a conversation with someone and it felt sticky, like something was not quite right? When you are stuck in something that you can't seem to work out, there is usually a truth with a lie attached. All you have to do is ask, **"What part of this is true and what part of this is a lie?"** and once you spot the lie, it suddenly becomes a truth and the stickiness disappears.

I once had a friend with all kinds of amazing talents and abilities with healing, so I asked him to come to an Access Consciousness class. My friend said, "I'd love to, but I can't afford it right now." I said I would gift the class to him because he was a friend. He said he would come to the class, but he didn't show up. Three days later I called him and he wouldn't take the call. I called again four days, five days and six days later, and he still wouldn't take the call. Finally I went to see him and asked, "How come you didn't come to the class?"

He said, "Well, I thought about it and I realized my true calling is to sell vitamins."

I was surprised, as this was a guy who had the ability to touch someone's body and heal things in a way few people could. I said, "Okay, fine, if that's your choice I totally get that." and we parted. However, I went away feeling something wasn't right and I kept asking, "What's wrong with this?" Finally I asked, "Okay, what's really going on? What is the truth here and what is the lie?"

Truth was "I have decided to sell vitamins." Okay. "My calling is to be a vitamin salesman." No, that was a lie. I realized that my friend's decision had to do with his wife, who didn't want her husband to become greater than she was. She was a chiropractor and he was a massage therapist in her office. That worked for her and that's where she wanted to keep things. She was the breadwinner. She was controlling him; he was younger than she was and she didn't want him to leave. He chose to allow that. They have since divorced because the relationship was based on contraction, not expansion. It had to die eventually.

As soon as I spotted that, all of my attention went off of it and I was able to let it go. I never saw my friend again. Why? My friend chose to lie to me, and when people lie to you, they have to go away.

Tool: Asking "Truth?"

When you ask, "Truth?" at the beginning of any question, the universe has to tell you what is true. It has to say *yes* or *no*. The person has to tell you the truth and if they don't, you will know they are lying. Even if you just think "truth" before you ask someone a question, you get to know what's true. So whenever you are questioning anybody who's selling something to you, or talking to somebody who wants to get something from you, ask, "Truth?" out loud or in your head, so you'll know if someone is lying to you.

How does this work? Dain and I once drove down to LA to buy a car. We walked into the place where the car was supposed to be for sale and the salesman said, "Oh, that car sold last week!" Well, we had called that morning and been told it wasn't sold, so I thought "Truth" and asked him to check again about the car

44

we had come to see. The salesman insisted that the car we had come for had been sold, and he said, "I'll show you one of these Porsches. I've done this to lots of people. They come in for another car and I sell them a Porsche." His true intention was exposed. He didn't even realize he had said it. Isn't that interesting? "I've done it to lots of people." Naturally we chose not to do business with that particular car salesman.

There have been a couple of attorneys who have learned this tool and they use it all the time. They always win their cases. A lady we know used it in her divorce settlement case. She would think "Truth" at her husband just before her attorney asked him a question, and he couldn't manage to lie successfully. Too bad!

You can use this with anyone. Just say "Truth" before you ask them any question and the truth will fall out of their mouth. It is a wonderful gift.

People try to do confrontation and reconciliation, but you don't want to reconcile, you want to know what's true. Don't be concerned if the other person never changes his or her point of view. Their changing their point of view is irrelevant—but knowing what they are truly going to do is relevant. It is more important to be aware than it is to speak the right thing. Don't do reconciliation or confrontation. Be aware. Trust the energy.

Do You Believe You Have to Tell the Truth?

Do you believe you have to tell the truth, the whole truth and nothing but the truth, so help you God? When you function from that belief, other people will lie to you and you will believe them! You believe that because you wouldn't lie, others will not lie to you, especially when they are your friends. Then when you find out later that one of your "friends" has blatantly lied to you,

you are shocked: "Oh my God, how come he lied to me? Doesn't he trust me?"

This is not about you. You assume people won't lie because you don't. Guess what? People lie all the time. Everybody lies—even you. If you don't believe that, ask yourself, "Who do I judge when I look in the mirror every morning?" That would be you. Are those judgments truth? No! So, you will lie to yourself and tell yourself what a pile of shit you are every day while believing nobody tells lies.

Chapter Seven

WHY DOESN'T THIS RELATIONSHIP WORK?

Have you tried to learn about relationship from the way it is done in contextual reality? Have you tried to discover what makes a good relationship based on what everybody else is doing? Do you see them doing all this intense emotional stuff and think they are having fun? Then you try it and you say, "Well, that wasn't fun for me, but everybody else is doing it so it must be fun!" Then you try it again and you say, "Well that wasn't fun for me. How come? What am I doing wrong? What am I not getting here? Everybody else is having such a good time with it!" The truth is that they are not having a good time but they keep promoting it like they are. What they really want is for you to choose to have a relationship so you can be as miserable as they are, which will prove that they were right to choose a relationship and make themselves that un-happy. Welcome to the world.

Wanting People to Like You

Most of us assume that people will like us when we shoot for being what people judge as "okay." The problem with this approach is that you don't get more people liking you when you do this; what you get is fewer people disliking you.

The truth is most people don't think about you. They cannot even be present in their own life, so how are they going to be present in yours? How can they see you? They don't remember your name, they don't remember where you are from or any of the things you consider important about you. What they remember are the things you do that irritate them.

If you are willing to be irritating or if you are willing to be whoever you are and not have the point of view that you want everybody to like you, it's amazing how many people will want to be around you. They will really like you no matter how irritating you are! When you are only willing to be liked by people, they don't want to have anything to do with you. People want to hang out with you when you are willing to be you.

Why? Because they recognize that you are being what they are refusing to be. They know that everybody else is playing according to the rules of cutting off parts of themselves so as not to be judged and to have people like them, so people who don't play by those rules are very attractive to them.

When you are willing to just be you, people don't have a place from which to judge you, because judgment doesn't have any effect on you. When you are willing to be you with no judgment of you, you can say, "Yeah, I know those rules, but they don't work for me. I'm going to be me, thanks very much." You are not coming from a place of forcing this on other people but from a place of "This is me right now. You can take it, you can leave it or you can judge it, and I'm going to keep on being me. And I'm okay with you being you too." If you truly like you and you don't change you for anybody else, then everybody is going to want to be around you.

Judgment as Connection

People use judgment to try to create an effect in your universe. They use it to create a connection or a separation from you. They look for how they can judge you in order to know how they are connected to you and to establish what the distance is between the two of you.

I learned this early on when I introduced my two best friends to each other. They decided to judge me and excommunicate me from the friendship and soon I was no longer a friend to either one of them. They used every judgment they had of me in order to find commonality between themselves and to eliminate me from their lives.

This is what some couples do as well. Have you ever had friends who were your friends only until they got married and then suddenly you became the single person who was no longer welcome in their life? That happens a lot, because couples want to hang out with couples; they don't want to hang out with single people because they have judgments about what single people might do with their partner. They only invite you to their house when they have someone they want to set you up with!

How do you use judgment to create connection? Many people believe that if you have the same judgments that they do, you must be like them; therefore they can like you. For example, all the people in church have the same judgments about what's right and what's wrong so they feel like a group. They believe they are liked when they are in that group and they can converse easily with each other because everyone has similar judgments.

Are you aware that you choose what to say to other people based on the judgments they have? It's as if you can push certain buttons and then a conversation comes out. You choose number 251 on the conversation menu, you push that button and the litany of judgment comes out. You call that your personality.

Did you know that you can pick those judgments out of other people's heads? You do it all the time so you know what to speak about in order to create a connection or a separation, as you choose. This is how most people control conversations.

Being Right

Often we don't ever question what we would actually like to have. It is your life you are spending. What would you like to choose? In the 10% reality, the point of view is you get the perfect relationship, you get kids, you get a dog, you get the white picket fence, and then you are going to live happily ever after. Do you think you are a loser if you don't have a relationship?

Isn't it interesting that this is how we run our lives? We will walk away from a relationship that is making us miserable and become happy; then we will go and look for another relationship to make ourselves miserable again. Ninety-five percent of people would rather have a bad relationship than no relationship at all. Why would you want a bad relationship? Because you don't want to be a loser. You don't want to be wrong.

When you choose rightness, you have to prove that whatever you think is right is right and whatever you have decided is wrong *is* wrong. Did you ever marry somebody or get into a relationship with somebody and then try to make it right that you chose that person? How many years did you spend trying to make it right? How long did you stay in order to prove that you had not made a wrong choice? Wow, that's smart, isn't it?

Most people in the world spend their life trying to prove that whatever they chose was right. Does that give you any freedom? No.

Tool: You Are Right, I Am Wrong

What if you had a choice between being right and being free? Which one would you choose? Ninety-nine percent of people surveyed chose "right." They would rather be right than free.

What is being free? Being free means you can choose anything. If you want true freedom then you have to be willing to be wrong.

My daughter Grace told me about a time she was out shopping for dresses with a friend. Grace had chosen a dress style and discovered there were only two of them in the store. The friend was a size larger than Grace, so Grace picked the one that was her size and gave her friend the one that was a size larger. The girl was upset that Grace had given her the larger size dress even though her body was physically larger. Grace was faced with a choice. She could keep the smaller dress and lose her friend or give up the smaller dress and keep the friend. What did she choose? She gave her friend the smaller dress.

For whatever reason, it was necessary for her friend to prove to Grace that she was the smaller size. If Grace had gone against that, it would have created a huge argument. Grace was willing to let her friend be right and she created freedom in her own universe with that choice. She also created not separating from her friend, which is what her friend would have chosen. How many times in your life have you insisted on being right rather than having the freedom that comes from not having a point of view?

How much of your life have you tried to prove that your point of view was right when it wasn't even your own point of view? You will try to prove that your point of view is right based on somebody else's point of view and the weird thing is that you will fight even harder for the points of view that aren't yours, which you have decided are right, than you will for your own point of view.

The one person you will not fight for is you. You will fight for the kids, you will fight for the family, you will fight for your country, but you won't fight for your own point of view. Why? You are trying to prove you are sane and normal like everyone else.

The truth is you are not normal. You are a humanoid. Humanoids are completely insane, because they don't fit! They are not normal; they do everything differently. Humanoids have a different point of view and they always want to believe they are wrong.

Chapter Eight

WHAT IF YOU ARE JUST DIFFERENT?

One of the more interesting discoveries we have made while working with people using the Access Consciousness tools has been the recognition that there are two different types of people on the planet. I began asking questions about the difference between the people who were seeking awareness of what could be different in their lives and the people who were not. The key difference seemed to be in the way they did judgment. There is one type of person who judges everybody and everything while believing he or she is always right. And there is another type of person who will judge himself or herself first and be convinced he or she must be wrong.

We call these two types of people humans and humanoids. I first became aware of this difference when Dain and I were sitting on a plane, watching two larger ladies get into their seats across the aisle. We noticed that these ladies were complaining about things the whole time with no concept that anything might have to do with them. For example, one lady said, "I can't believe that they keep making these airplane seats smaller and smaller." The idea that perhaps she was getting larger was nowhere in her universe. She was convinced the airline was doing something to her. I was curious about this behavior and I asked, "What's different about these women?" The answer was, "Oh, They're human!"

I asked, "We are all human too, right?" The answer was No!

I then asked, "If they are human, what are we?" I was stunned by the awareness that the women on the plane were the humans, and Dain and I were the ones who were different. That is how I first became aware of humanoids.

A humanoid is someone who is always looking for how something can be better. Humanoids will always do judgment of themselves in pursuit of this something better. They are always saying (or thinking), "How come I don't fit? Why don't I feel like everybody else? How come I can't seem to do anything right?"

Humans, on the other hand, have the point of view that they are always right, everybody else is wrong, and if you just do things their way, everything will be fine. Anything that requires them to change is wrong. The human point of view is that there are no other possibilities. You will know whether someone is human if they sit in judgment of you nonstop, 24/7.

Access Consciousness work is usually a matter of getting people out of the maze they are stuck in, but there are some people who seem to have no way out of their maze. They're the humans.

Do you recognize anyone you know in these descriptions? Do you recognize yourself? It is important to understand that this awareness about humans and humanoids is not about judging one kind of person as better than the other. This information is presented solely to help you stop judging yourself as wrong and to help you to see that you are just different.

Humanoid Characteristics

Humanoids are chameleons in disguise. They are infinitely ad-justable. You can change your color to fit any scene but you think that is wrong. How many times have you been told, "You are such a faker; I can't believe you are doing that." Is it wrong to be a cha-meleon? No. It is a brilliant capacity. Claim it, own it, acknowl-edge it, and start doing it more, because you can make yourself fit anywhere. Just don't assume that you actually fit anywhere; instead know that you can fit. And start asking some questions like, "Do I really wish to fit here?"

Have you been told you are too much? Do people tell you that you can't possibly do as many projects as you do, yet you always get everything done? As a humanoid, you have excessive energy that you have to put somewhere. You get yourself into trouble if you don't have at least five things going on at all times in your life. Have you noticed that when you do more, you always get things done even more easily, and when you do less, you create trauma and drama and things don't get done nearly as easily?

People may say you have OCD (obsessive compulsive disorder), but what you really are is an OCC. You are an Obsessive Com-pulsive Creator. And if you don't have enough going on in your life at all times, you become an OCCC, an Obsessive Compulsive Creator of Crap.

Humanoids Procrastinate

Humanoids think they are procrastinators because they put things off until the last minute. When you were in high school and you had term papers to do, would you start the project at 11:30 the night before the paper was due? Even the ones where the teacher told you to start three months in advance to get it done, did you still start at 11:30 at night? And did you get it done and still get a grade that worked for you? That is a humanoid trait. It is one way you can prove you are powerful.

Why don't you make your life easier? Instead of waiting for the last minute to prove you are powerful, what if you just got powerful all the time and got the work done before it was due? What if you got everything done before it was necessary to do it? Do you think that would be boring?

It actually wouldn't be boring, because it would open the doors to all kinds of things you can add to your life that would allow you to move out of the 10%! The only way you can keep yourself in the 10% is to do things at the last minute! Your whole life is about putting out fires in the 10% realm; you don't ever allow yourself to experience the space of the 990%. What if you gave up being a fire fighter?

Humanoids at Work

A human point of view is, "This is the way we've always done it, this is the way we will always do it, this is the way it should be done and you are wrong if you don't do it this way." If you are humanoid, you will have been accused of working too fast and making everybody look bad. You will have been accused of not doing things right because you want to change everything.

Humanoids will take a job and within three hours to three days, they will have worked out the whole thing and know exactly what it takes to change it and make it better. Then they will be bored. They will resort to having to change the job or getting into trouble to make it more interesting.

Humanoids figure out what they like to do in life by doing different things until they don't like them any more. As I said, this usually takes about three weeks, so they have a hard time putting in twenty years. Have you done enough of what you don't desire and don't require? Will you finally acknowledge that you know what you don't desire now? Would you claim, own and acknowledge that you have no bloody clue what you do desire? Realize it is a humanoid thing to figure out what you would like to do by doing things that bore you to tears so you will not choose to do them again.

Money doesn't matter to a humanoid. You like money but what you *really* like is creating and generating things. When you create something that's really cool and somebody actually gets it, you won't want to charge them for it. In fact, it's almost impossible to ask for the money and 90% of the time, you will give them a discount as well. As a humanoid you have got to be willing to have the money too! Giving something away does not make people appreciate it.

Humanoids Are "Nice"

One of the characteristics of humanoids is being too nice. The thing about being a humanoid is that if somebody is mean to you, you will say, "Oh, they must be having a bad day." No, people are mean just because they can be. As a humanoid, because you wouldn't choose to be that mean without a very good reason, you will try to justify that they must have had something terrible happen to them that would make them choose that. Nope. People choose what they choose because they can, not for any other reason.

If you are in a relationship with a human, the human wants you to be their doormat. So now what are you going to do? As a humanoid you have to learn to become bluntly honest with yourself. Ask yourself, "I am choosing this for what reason?" Not "I am choosing this because it makes my partner's life better, because it is good for him or her, or because it is going to work out better this way. If I give up me and divorce me everything's going to be greater."

Have you been trying to be good so you can get the good stuff in life? Do you feel you have to live a life of piety and purity and never do mean and ugly things to others? As a humanoid, you want to be a moralist. Do you realize that only humanoids are moral? Humans will always lie, cheat and steal. The golden rule, "Do unto others as you would have done unto you" only works on humanoids. They are the only ones that will follow that insane point of view. Humans will do anything to anyone they choose and know that they are right.

Humans are the ones that say, "Man, I love being a Catholic. I go to confession and I get absolved of all my sins and then I can go out and have sex with another girl the next week and go to the priest and get absolved of my sins again."

Humanoids Try Not to Be Aware

Humanoids sit in so much judgment of themselves that they tend to do alcohol and drugs to turn it off or change it. It doesn't work. Humanoids are also very aware psychically and they pick up everybody else's thoughts, feelings and emotions, so they use drugs and alcohol as a way of trying to turn off the information they receive. All that does is exponentialize their awareness. You can't actually access your awareness from that place, so you think it is working because it tones everything down temporarily—but it doesn't actually work at all.

If somebody's human, it doesn't mean they don't have psychic abilities, and it doesn't mean they don't have unique capacities in life. Human doesn't mean dumb and stupid. Many psychic astrologers, tarot card readers, and aura readers are human. They just approach things from the human perspective, which is that you are wrong. You are wrong, I am right and you should change. Being a humanoid, you buy into it and you assume that because they say they are right, they must be right. You think, "Well, maybe I am not right. Maybe I am just being judgmental; maybe I am wrong about this."

Humanoids Who Wish They Were Human

There are some humanoids who are desperately seeking to be human. You can recognize humanoids who are desperately trying to be human because they age themselves beyond their years. They look older than they should look. They try so hard to bend, fold, staple and mutilate themselves into this reality that they die from the effort of it. They either kill themselves quickly, age themselves dynamically or they change; those are the three options for them.

You may see that as sad, but it is a choice and it is a kindness to be in allowance of their choice. Their choice is just an interesting point of view. Why would you try to change them? Stop thinking you can save people. What if you were to let them be as they choose to be? They want to die, and that is their choice, isn't it?

There was a lady who had a dog that she kept in the house all the time because she was afraid that it would get run over. The dog hated being in the city; it wanted to be a country dog, but she wouldn't give it away to somebody who had a farm. One day her son went out to collect the mail and forgot to close the door. The dog ran out into the street directly in front of a car and was killed. The dog was willing to commit suicide because it didn't want to be in the city. What about a humanoid that really wants to be a human? Are they going to commit suicide? Yes, in one form or another, so why not let them? If they are not willing to choose what they are, why don't you let them choose what they choose instead?

Humanoids Never Give Up

The nice thing about being a humanoid is when somebody says, "You can't." Humanoids respond with, "I'll bet I can," and they do it, every time. This is the sign of a humanoid. Someone tells you not to do something and you just have to do it—even if it is the wrong thing to do—just to prove that you can. All the great art and literature and all the significant innovations in the world are created by humanoids.

This is not reverse psychology; this is humanoid. Reverse psychology only works on humanoids. It does not work on humans. When you say, "You can't do that" to a human, the human says, "You are right. I don't want to, anyway." A humanoid will say, "What do you mean I can't do it? You wanna bet? Watch me." That is a humanoid perspective. If you don't believe it, look at your own life.

Another thing about humanoids is that they won't give up. As long as there is a breath of life in their body, they never give up. It is part of being humanoid. Have you ever tried to give up in one form or another? Can an infinite being really give up? No. Not as long as you are still breathing.

Humans and Humanoids in Relationships

Humanoid women do not want to stay at home and take care of the kids. That is way too boring for them. Most humanoid women need at least three men in their life to fulfill what they personally desire. They need one for social events, one for family events and one to spend the evening with, watching TV and eating popcorn. And of course, they get to have sex with all three of them. For some women, two more men would be helpful; one to go dancing with and one do things like going for walks in the woods. It is insane to think it can all come in one package.

Humanoid men are the nesters in relationships. They like having a nice, calm, cool and collected place to live. They like having a place that is aesthetic and pleasing to them.

Humanoid women have been told they are supposed to be nurturing and caring and that their role is taking care of men. Do you humanoid women actually like that idea? Or do you want to say, "Get your own dinner; I've worked hard today, so clean up after yourself. I don't want to do your laundry; I wish you would do your own laundry." As a humanoid woman, you might want to ask for a man that is willing to be the wife for you. "What would it take for a man to come along who was willing to take care of me?" You even don't have to have a relationship. What if you just wanted to have someone in your life that was fun for you to hang out with or fun to have sex with?

Human women are quite different. They have the point of view that men should do what they tell them. For a human woman, nurturing and caring for her man means criticizing him, telling him how wrong he is and then demanding sex. That's harsh, isn't it? Even after discovering all this information about human women, Dain and I thought it couldn't be true.

But then there was a *20/20* program on TV that had followed two (human) families as representative of the sex life of married couples. One couple had three children, the other couple had two children, and both women were angry because their husbands would no longer have sex with them. The human point of view is that you are supposed to have 2.5 children and then quit having sex. In both of the families on the *20/20* program, the men quit having sex with their mates after they had two or three children. They didn't find their wives attractive any more; they were only willing to masturbate and were no longer willing to copulate. The women were critical, mean and nasty, and wondered why their men would not sleep with them.

Interestingly enough, one of the things that we became aware of about humanoids is that they do copulation for fun whereas humans do copulation for procreation.

Make-up sex does not exist for a humanoid. It only exists for humans. If a woman judges her humanoid man and then expects to go to bed with him, she will be disappointed. He will be angry for at least three days after he's been judged. Head through the headboard sex also doesn't exist for humanoids, but that is a turn on for humans. The humanoid perspective of copulation is "long, slow, take your time, turn me on, let me turn you on; let's see how many juices we can get flowing here."

Human women want men to do everything for them. They say things like, "Do what I tell you" and "I don't know what your problem is. Stop wasting your time with all those weird things you are into. Sit down, watch some football, drink a beer and be happy." That's a human woman.

Humanoid women have to have adventures. If they don't have adventures, they don't want to stay. If you are with a humanoid woman, encourage her to go off into the world and do something for herself, then she will come back and be really happy to be home with you for a time.

The humanoid woman loves to conquer the world. Her man should send her out every day with, "Hey, can I get you breakfast before you go out to conquer the world, honey?" She will think you are just the greatest thing in the world. When she gets home she'll say, "Come here, lover…" Things won't be as happy if you are trying to prove you are the competition. Men have been told they need to be the aggressors, but are they truly aggressive? Not by choice. Humanoid women like playing the bad cop and the tough guy. Humanoid men are good at being the good cop, the nice guy, the equalizer.

Have you chosen humans to be in relationship with? If you married somebody who is human and you have children, your children are humanoids. They will eventually rebel against human reality.

Chapter Nine

WHAT ABOUT LOVE, ROMANCE AND MARRIAGE?

Humanoids are romantics of magnitude. They love the romance of the seduction, dancing, looking into each other's eyes, drinking wine in soft candlelight, walking outdoors together and having long meaningful conversations. Unfortunately they always create a relationship when the romance is really the only part they like. They enjoy the romance and then they say, "Oh, maybe I'm supposed to be with this person forever."

It is hard for a humanoid to do long-term monogamy because they get bored easily. Have you had a relationship that at a certain point became so boring you thought you would die if you had to stay there? But then you didn't want to acknowledge that you were bored, so you tried to make you wrong in some way and then tried to rekindle the romance somehow?

The Romance of Unrequited Love

The classic romantic love story is unrequited love. Are you doing unrequited love as though that is the truth of you? Do you only love those who will not love you? Do you refuse to receive the love of those who will actually lay down their life for you?

This is being a romantic. A romantic thinks that things ought to be the way they ought to be instead of the way they are. Do you look at the love stories where everybody finally gets together in the end and everything ends up right and you cry, because that's the way it ought to be, but that isn't the way it is? Do you keep trying to live your life as though it's going to turn out like the book? Like the movie or the romance novel?

The problem with being a humanoid is you believe in romance because you know it's the way things ought to turn out. But instead of looking at it and asking, "Okay, that's not what is showing up here. Where is the lie?" you say, "If I finally just get it right, it will turn out the way it 'ought' to. I just have to try harder."

Trying harder doesn't work. There's only one thing you want hard in life—and it isn't your trying.

What Is Love?

When people say, "I love you," what do they mean? How many definitions are there for love? More than a billion? Probably! When someone says, "I love you," what do you hear? What are they saying? Do you have a clue? Or do you hear what agrees with your own definition of love?

What people say and what is their truth is not the same thing. My ex-wife used to say, "I love you more than anybody in the world" even though she would judge me, say mean and vicious things to me and make sure she didn't support me in any way. It was because she loved me. But that was true for her— because that is what she thought love was. She believed her parents must love her even though they were mean and vicious and never supported her.

The difficulty is that, even if somebody's really mean, you will still care about them. Even if they do mean, vicious things to you continuously, you still care about them. You may try not to, and you may think it would be easier if you cut yourself off from them, but it doesn't work for you because caring is part of who you are as humanoid.

What if you gave up love and went for gratitude instead?

Gratitude has no judgment. In love there can be judgment but in gratitude judgment cannot exist. You can even be grateful for somebody who's a liar. There is no judgment of the fact they lie; there's only an awareness that they lie. I can be grateful for liars because I always know they will lie to me. I don't anticipate that they will tell me the truth. I am grateful for the fact that they are liars because I know I don't have to trust them, I don't have to have blind faith that they are going to tell me the truth.

When you have gratitude for someone, it is expansive. When you have love for somebody it can be judgmental. In the metaphysical community, they talk about unconditional love. Unconditional love only works as long as you don't do something "wrong," then your unconditional love becomes very conditional.

You don't have to live on the basis of your emotions. Most people try to prove that they love you by being highly emotional. "I am being amazing because I have such strong emotions." What does that mean? It is always a proof that the emotions are being something greater than you. What if you were simply grateful for the people who come into your life?

Try saying, "I am grateful for you. I am grateful for who you are and what you are." That is the truth of what you are talking about when you say, "I love you." When you tell a kid you are grateful for them, they know what you are talking about. When you say, "I love you," they wait for the hand that is going to spank them because whenever their parents spank them, they say, "I am doing this because I love you." That creates confusion, not love.

Passionate Relationships

Do you really want to have a passionate relationship? The difficulty with passion is that it comes from the Greek word for *suffering*. One of the definitions of *passion* is the *suffering of Christ on the Cross.* Do you want to be crucified on the cross that is your relationship? Do you feel you need to suffer for love?

Have you ever been in a passionate relationship where you couldn't keep your hands off somebody and they couldn't keep their hands off you? How did that relationship end? You probably found that it ended badly. That's because passion is about suffering. When you have a passionate relationship with somebody, you may wish to ask this question: "Is it my turn to kill them or is it their turn to kill me?"

You don't want passion in relationship; you want the joy and the peace of a contributive, nurturing, expansive relationship. The trouble is hardly anyone wants something that is easy and generative and contributory to their life; they want *passion!*

Being a Couple

There is no such thing as a couple. That's the biggest lie you create—that you can be a couple. No. You are two individuals who have the capacity to live together. When you make yourself into a couple, you create a limitation, because anything that doesn't fit your definition of *couple* has to go away.

In order for people to be a couple, they have to be in a constant state of judgment as to whether it's okay for them to be "this" because they are a couple, or whether it's not okay for them to be "this" because they are a couple.

That Special One for You

That "special one" is a myth. The reality is you have at least eight thousand special ones. Doesn't that make you feel lighter? How does it get any better than that? You don't want to look for the special one for you. What you want to look for are people who are vibrationally compatible with you.

There is a vibrational compatibility that exists between people who have a really great relationship. They are so vibrationally compatible that you couldn't imagine them not being with the other person.

You can have that vibrational compatibility with someone of the same sex but it doesn't require you to copulate with them. And if you do happen to copulate with them, cool! That's just a bonus; it is not a requirement of vibrational compatibility.

Most people want one person who is the whole package, but that is an insanity that contextual reality perpetrates on us. You could have vibrational compatibility with a friend who was just wonderful and you could also have vibrational compatibility with someone you copulate with and play with that way. Why look for it all in one person?

If you look for everything in one person, how much judgment do you have to do? It takes a huge amount of energy. And is any one person perfectly complimentary to you? No. Yet we keep trying to create this ideal special one as though somehow this must be true.

Do You Wish to Be Married?

Marriage is something that we invented somewhere along the way. It was invented to make sure we kept our property in the correct family line. It was a product of the church and state and provided a way to transfer property. The whole purpose of marriage was to ensure your progeny would inherit your wealth. That was the sum total of what it was originally about— then it became "meaningful," which is the thing that drives you crazy. There is nothing wrong with marriage or relationships when they work, but this whole thing of shooting for marriage is usually about programming. You are programmed to go from childhood to getting a job to getting married, and that is not choice.

The truth is that most humanoids will be grateful for a relationship for about eight weeks. When the pheromones stop, so do they. Here is another way you could do relationship. You could go to the other person and say, "I'd really like to have a relationship with you. Can I move in with you for eight weeks and after that we'll know if we want to be together longer, but plan on me leaving in eight weeks." They will be totally present with you for eight weeks and then when the eight weeks is up, make sure you leave. Don't stay after eight weeks just because you think you will get sex continuously. After eight weeks the sex will quit. That's just the way it works. An infinite being would have a long-term relationship for what reason?

We're trying to give you the picture of where you sit so you have choice instead of making yourself wrong for the point of view that it's just for fun, which is actually more real to you than marriage. This is about becoming aware that you like the romance but you don't like the relationship; you don't like the washing clothes and washing dishes part.

Would you really like to stay with the same person for long periods of time? Is there anybody you want to spend all your time with? No. A psychology professor once asked his class to write down their answers to this question: "If you were madly in love with somebody, what percentage of your time would you want to spend with them?" The majority of the answers ranged from 75% to 80%. Out of twenty-four hours how much is 75% of your time? Eighteen hours!

Would you really want to spend eighteen hours with anyone? You usually sleep eight hours a day, which is time you avoid even spending with yourself, so how does the idea of spending eight hours every day, one third of your life, with someone else, sound to you? Exciting or boring?

Think about the work colleagues that you spend most of your day with; how many of them do you like to spend time with after work? Not many of them, right? In reality, about two and a half hours a day is enough time to spend with anybody. If you spent two and a half hours a day of quality time with someone, would that be enough? Yes. For those of us who have children, about twenty minutes of quality time is enough. After that you get bored and want to do something that is fun for you.

Long-term relationship is not an easy gig for us humanoids unless you have a truly unique person to be with. That would be someone who's always willing to change and always willing to see what else they can conquer, what else they can change and what else they can be. These people are fun to be with because at the end of the day they are different people. Who you wake up with and who you go to bed with are two different people.

Very few people are willing to do that; they try to stay in the same box they think the other person wants, which for you as a humanoid, gets boring after about two days. You start to think, "I know I'm supposed to love this, so why do I hate it?"

Partners who are continuously willing to change have amazing communion together. They don't limit each other; they actually expand each other and contribute to each other's lives. They help the other person become more of who they are. They don't try to maintain consistency nor do they try to maintain the same "be-ingness." They do not attempt to maintain ownership of the other person and they do not do the jealousy thing of not wanting that person to change and become greater out of the fear that he or she will go away or find somebody else.

The problem is when you try to get somebody not to leave you, the person who leaves is you.

Till Death Do Us Part

Being a typical humanoid, when you make a commitment to something, it's forever. When you say, "Till death do us part" that's what it really is. Whether you get divorced or not is irrelevant. You will do "till death do us part" no matter what it takes.

71

You go into a marriage as one person then become another person that your partner doesn't like. You get out of the marriage because your partner doesn't like you and you don't like him or her, and then you are back to being the person you like. You don't understand why the other person doesn't like you. That's because you didn't keep your commitment. You were supposed to take care of him or her forever. And so you will, because you are one of those stupid humanoid people who keep your word.

The trouble is that you as a being never die, and you have made about eight billion of these promises around the world. Every time you make a new one you have another "Till death do us part" point of view. You can choose to stop doing that by giving up all your oaths, vows, swearings, fealties, comealties, commitments, and promises to take care of someone forever.

It is a great gift to give up those things, for you and for the other person. Because then they'll start taking care of themselves and when they start to take care of themselves, they might pull somebody into their life who they would really like to have.

Would you like to give up your oaths, vows, swearings, fealties, comealties, commitments, and promises to take care of this person forever? *Everything that is, times a godzillion will you destroy and uncreate it all, please? Yes? Thank you. Right and wrong, good and bad, POD and POC, all nine, shorts, boys and beyonds.*

What was that we just said? This phrase is what we call the Access Consciousness Clearing Statement. This is the way we clear areas that are keeping us stuck.

Chapter Ten

THE CLEARING STATEMENT

What is the basis of the universe? Energy. Every particle of the universe has energy and consciousness. Energy is the substance by which transformation occurs. Energy is present, mutable and changeable upon request.

The walls appear to be solid but science will tell us that this is not actually true. There is apparently more space than particles in what we call "solid" matter. The molecules of the wall are moving and vibrating and we are just not at a vibration that would allow us to pass through them. So if there's a blockage in our life, the same principles apply. We have slowed everything down so that we cannot vibrate equal to it and move through it. Wherever we have these kinds of blockages in life, the clearing statement allows us to undo them so we can have a different choice.

Tool: The Clearing Statement

We think words have meaning because we attach meaning to them, but they are actually an energy. The only reason we can translate energy into words is because the energy of the word and the word itself are the same energy.

These are the words that make up the clearing statement.

Everything that is, times a godzillion, I destroy and uncreate it all. Right and wrong, good and bad, POD and POC, all nine, shorts, boys and beyonds.

What are we doing when we use these words? When we ask questions about something we call up the energy that has us locked into it and then we destroy and uncreate it all with the clearing statement. We ask the energy to go to the point of creation (POC) and the point of destruction (POD) so that it disintegrates and goes away. The words in the clearing statement are a kind of short-speak for the energy being asked for. We say the clearing statement as words but it is the energy that changes things, not the words.

You don't have to understand it for it to work, but if you want to know more, there is a complete explanation of the clearing statement in the back of this book.

Access Consciousness is different from most of the things you have done, because we are not giving you our answers and trying to get you to change your mind. We all know that doesn't work. You are the only one who can unlock the points of view that have you trapped. Access Consciousness can give you the tools that make it easy by showing you how to change the energy.

Whatever we choose puts the energy of the universe, the energy of consciousness, into action and that shows up as our life. This

74

is what your life looks like in this very moment. Literally the first language is energy. Everything you say, everything you think and everything you do generates what occurs in your life.

Is there good energy and bad energy—or is everything just energy? Everything is just energy. It is only our judgment that makes anything so. There is no energy that is unavailable to us if we choose to be aware of it.

To use the clearing statement, ask a question designed to bring up the energy of what has you trapped including all the crap built on it or hiding behind it, then say or read the clearing statement to clear it and change it. The more you run these clearing statements, the deeper they go and the more layers and levels they can unlock for you.

Here is an example of how it works.

Remember we were talking about passion in relationships and how that creates suffering? Well, you can solve a lot of relationship angst with this particular question if you are willing to go with it and see what feels light for you. Asking the question brings up an energy which you will be aware of and then you can clear it with the clearing statement.

First ask, *"Have I killed them more or have they killed me more?"* Which feels lighter? Now ask, *"Whose turn is it to kill the other one in this lifetime? Theirs or mine?"* Which feels lighter? Now you can clear it by saying: *"I revoke, recant, rescind, reclaim, renounce, denounce, destroy and uncreate all my commitments to continue this vendetta through all eternity. Right and wrong, good and bad, POD and POC, all nine, shorts, boys and beyonds."*

The clearing statement may seem nonsensically wordy. It is designed to short-circuit your mind so that you can see what choices you have available. If you can't figure it out, go with the energy of it. You can't do this wrong. You will have a different way of functioning as a result of using the clearing statement.

Ending Up Where You Started

Look at your life and see how many times you have played the same story over and over with different characters. You keep asking yourself, "How come I keep ending up back here?" Well, 90% of what you are run by is based on decisions you made in another lifetime. The clearing statement will start to undo that so you can have a different choice.

When you use these tools and processes, you start to generate a future life that's different. You will no longer be the effect of people, things, events or anything else. You will choose to be something that generates different possibilities instead of something that fights for or against things. If you are always fighting for or against, you are doing polarity and when you are locked into polarity, you have no choice.

The POD and POC is about going back and unlocking anywhere you took a polarized point of view, which requires an enormous amount of energy to hold in place. When you unlock that point of view, you no longer have the need to hold onto that energy. This means you now have that energy available to generate your life. The more you are willing to change, the more POD and POC you do, and the more energy accumulates behind you like an avalanche. You have more energy because you are not fighting against that point of view, and because you are no longer using your energy against you or keeping it locked in. It is now available to generate your life. So when you say, "I'd like to have that" it goes out into the universe and invites that thing you desire to come in to you—and it does!

When you POC and POD something, the particular area you are dealing with will get clearer and there will be greater ease in it. It is instantaneous. Then after a while, something else will come up and start bugging you like a yappy dog and you realize, "Oops, there's something else here I have to deal with." Dain says that he has been using Access tools and processes for over ten years and every day there's a dog that yaps. So he keeps looking at different areas of life and things keep getting better. He keeps having more fun, more money and more of everything he asks for. Don't use these tools unless you desire your life to change, okay?

"Ask and you shall receive" is one of the truths presented in the Bible. It is one of the tools in the Bible that actually works. And it also explains why the clearing statement works.

Losing Your Mind

Be grateful if this expression doesn't make logical sense to your mind. Your mind can only define the limitations of your reality; it is a calculating system that only defines what you already know. We're here to wipe out your mind and give you a clean slate.

Once you wipe out your mind as the regulating system of your life, you get to function from knowing. Your mind gets in the way of knowing. We've all had moments, when with the snap of your fingers, you knew everything, and you said, "Wow, that's so cool." Can you think yourself into those positions? No. If your mind truly worked, wouldn't you have been able to think your way out of all these messes already? When you *know* something, it's instantaneous and it does not require figuring out.

Your insane mind has all the answers to how you create the limitations of your reality. Your logical mind justifies everything you do and does nothing to create the infinite possibilities.

When You Change, the People Around You Change

The funny part about this stuff is you do all the work and everybody around you changes. When you change your points of view, the people you are connected to also change, often without knowing it.

There was a lady who had done many Access Consciousness classes and one day she said to me, "I can't believe it! You said I would do all the work and everybody around me would change and it's true! For the last five years I have gone to family reunions and usually within ten minutes there has been a fistfight and somebody goes away mad. Nobody ever talks to anybody and everybody always hates everybody else by the end of day. Well, I just went to a family reunion and this time everybody got along, everybody was happy and I talked with my Dad, who I have never talked to for longer than fifteen minutes, for an hour and a half. It was the most wonderful event our family has ever had and everybody said so. But the only person who has done anything different is me!"

It is weird how this works, but it does. You are asking, "What changed?" The answer is: "You did!"

Chapter Eleven

CHOOSING TO CHANGE

We have a free will universe here, which means you can choose anything. You can choose that which is contributory and expansive to your life and you can choose that which is contractive and eliminates things from your life. How does that work?

When I married my ex-wife, she said she didn't like my friends so we were only allowed to associate with her friends. By making the choice to marry her, I eliminated all my old friends. Smart? No. When I made the choice to marry her, I didn't realize she would demand that we have nothing to do with my friends. Her point of view was none of them were worth knowing. I could no longer talk to friends I had for years unless I made a point of going outside the marriage and having a relationship with them that had nothing to do with her. That was the only way I could have a relationship with any of them.

I finally got to the point where I realized I didn't exist in the relationship with my wife. I would call her and say, "Hey, can we have so-and-so over for dinner?" She would respond with, "No I don't like him." Then she would call me back ten minutes later and say, "I invited my friend so-and-so to come spend the weekend. You don't mind, do you?" I began to realize my point of view didn't count. What I would like was irrelevant. Over time I had divorced more and more of me in order to make the relationship work for her. There was no allowance of my choices in her universe.

Any time you make a choice, you add things and you also eliminate things from your life. Look at the choices you make and ask, "What does this choice eliminate from my life? What does it add to my life?" Be aware of what you are choosing.

People don't tend to make choices about relationships from consciousness; they tend to choose from other people's points of view. That is like wearing clothes that don't suit your body. Do they make your body look good—or do they make your body look ridiculous? They make it look ridiculous, yet you assume they make it look good because everybody is wearing clothes like that.

You look at everybody else and say, "They seem able to function here and I don't feel I function here. I don't feel like I belong here. I don't know where I fit; I don't know how to do these things. Maybe these other people understand something I don't." You try to figure out how to do things the way they do them so you can get something right in life, only you don't have the success they have. Why? Because you are making choices based on someone else's point of view.

Tool: How Did I Create This?

Every choice you make creates your reality. Every choice you make creates the life you are currently living and it creates your future. If you are not happy with what you are creating, ask, **"How did I create this?** Where was that ten seconds of unconsciousness I chose that brought this into existence?"** When you get that awareness, you have two choices. You can do judgment of it—and destroy all possibility of creating something different or you can ask a question like, "What would I like to change about this?" and be different. Your choice creates the difference.

Choosing the Cesspool

Do you know what a cesspool is? A cesspool is where all the turds and piss go after they are flushed down the toilet. It's a pool of floating turds and piss. This is where the majority of people live, in the 10% cesspool.

Next door is the 990% clear pool. For some reason, nobody is in the clear pool. So would you like to continue to swim in the cesspool or would you be willing to get out and try the 990% pool? The 990% pool has lots of space and lots of clean clear water. There is no chlorine in it because you don't have to put chlorine in a pool when nobody's pissing in it.

The weird part of this scenario is that it is so simple. Climb out of the cesspool, take two steps and get into the clear pool. But we act like, "I can't! I just can't! I can't ever get out of the cesspool!"

Why not? Well, all of your friends are in the cesspool. Why would you want to leave the other turds behind? We are trying to make this very graphic in the hope that you will get the image and it will stick with you in some way so you can say, "Oh, family, cesspool, okay, excuse me. I am going over here. I am going to swim in this clear pool. You guys enjoy yourselves. Bye, see you later!"

The cesspool is the comfort zone. If you are swimming with turds, you know you are alive and all is as it should be. If you want to choose that, it's okay. Does it make you happy when you do it? No? So don't choose it.

Unfortunately, moving into the clear pool will require one thing of you: the willingness to take advantage of the people in the cesspool. Taking advantage of those that are swimming in the cesspool is moving into the clear pool. You have to be willing to take advantage because otherwise you have to swim with the turds. Have you had enough of swimming with the turds?

Do you have the point of view that by choosing the clear pool you are not being kind or you are not doing the right thing? Whose point of view is that? If you are functioning from the 990%, you will always be beyond where everybody else functions from, so you will be taking advantage no matter what you do. Everything you do will be taking advantage because you will not have a tough life. You will not be choosing the cesspool. You will be choosing the clear pool automatically if you start functioning from the 990%.

Do you realize how much work you are doing to not be that 990%?

Rescuing Others from the Cesspool

Are you trying to rescue everybody from the cesspool? Do you believe they are drowning and need you to help them? What usually happens when you try to rescue a drowning person? They pull you back in and you both drown. So you would want to do that for what reason?

People in the cesspool like being in the cesspool! They love it! Every time you try to rescue them, they get together and they hold on to each other so they have enough weight to pull you in too. That is what you are going to get when you try to save people.

First of all, did you ask them a question like, "Do you want to be saved?" Did they ask you a question like, "Will you save me?" No. So if you try to save them when they haven't asked you a question, they will drown you in the cesspool of love. People choose what they choose and you have to understand that people choose what they have. You even have to let people die if that's what they are choosing. That's the way to stay in the clear pool.

I have two sons that have gone through major drug problems and both of them have been in positions where death was just a hair's breadth away. One of them has done such damage to his body that if he lives another five years it will be a miracle. He has done massive amounts of drugs of one sort or another to the point that he actually had his heart stop. It only started again when he hit the floor. That was self-CPR, a pound to the heart, boom! I did my best to show my son there was a different possibility, but he didn't want to choose it. I am clear that my son has chosen to live his life the way it is.

It is his life, not mine. I can't make him do anything. There is sadness for me that this would be my son's choice, but I find it sad that many people choose the things they choose. I see so many kinds of people choosing things that will destroy their life, destroy their money, destroy their relationships, and it is always sad to me to see somebody do that. But it will not stop me from choosing the 990% space.

It may seem like people in the cesspool don't know how to get out. But it's not that they don't know how to get out; they don't know there is another choice. They can't see that clear pool over there because nobody has told them it exists and because everybody's saying, "Don't look!"

Finding the 990% of You

Are you willing to go on the adventure of life or would you rather go on the predictable vacation called Cesspool 101? Have you been enjoying the cesspool you are currently swimming in? No? Why not try the clear pool even though you have no idea what it is going to be like? There might be champagne in that other pool. There might be good things in that other pool. You don't know what it is going to be. Would you rather stay where you know what's going on?

You may be someone who has to have a map before you will even start on the journey. You may have never, ever gone on a journey without knowing in advance where you are heading. What if it was way more fun to go on a journey that has never existed before?

Think of it like going into space. You are going to a space where you might find things you never knew existed. Mostly what you are going to find is the other 9,000 pieces of you that you have never seen. You have been taking one piece out of the 10,000

84

pieces of you and you have been living as that; and that has been the 10% of your life. You have another 990% available, which is another 9,999 pieces of you that you could find if you were willing to go on the journey.

You can say, "But I don't have a space suit. And I haven't been trained to go into space. Where's the rocket and who is going to lift it off? Where are all the people who will support me when I get up in the air? Who will get me back down again when I get there?" The truth is that you don't need a space suit and you don't need a rocket ship; you just need more of you.

What if you could move beyond where anybody else was capable of living? Would that be of interest to you? Would that be more fun than what you are currently doing? Would that be more fun than anybody else is having? You would never know what was going to come next, which means you would never be bored again.

Would that be exciting? Or have you bought the lie that it would be fearful for you to not know what the next moment brings? What about the joy of living? What is more fun? Having sex with the same person over and over again in the same way, or trying new ways and new people?

I'm Afraid

We're sorry to tell you this, but fear is a total lie. You do not have an ounce of fear. Here is the proof. When there is an emergency situation, do you fall apart and run away? Or do you get calm, cool, collected and handle what has to be handled? You get calm, cool and collected and handle what has to be handled, don't you? That is because you have no fear. If you truly had fear you would fall apart or run away in an emergency.

You make yourself 10% and when there is an emergency situation, you step up to 12%. When you do this, everything begins to move slowly and you handle everything so it all gets straightened out. This is why grannies can pick up trucks and pull out little children with one hand. This is the power and the potency that is available to us all—but we only step into it in an emergency.

You take care of everything until it is okay for you to let go of holding onto everything. The emotion that you sometimes experience as shock after a trauma is not usually yours. It is what you have taken out of others so they can be calm, cool, collected and handle things too. If you go through a trauma situation and you don't acknowledge the potency you were being, you will often create the lie in your universe that you are a fearful and afraid person.

Would you like to acknowledge now all the potency you've displayed a thousand times over when you thought you must have been afraid (because everybody said you had to be afraid) even though you were not fearful? Would you also acknowledge that you stepped into the potency of the 12% to 15% in that situation then misidentified and misapplied that you were afraid because you didn't acknowledge that potency? *Everything that is times a godzillion, will you destroy and uncreate it all? Yes? Thank you. Right and wrong, good and bad, POD and POC, all nine, shorts, boys and beyonds.*

What would it be like if you were the power that would give you everything you have ever looked for in you and never found?

The only place you are going to find YOU is in the clear pool. All you can find in the cesspool are the other turds floating around. Have you been looking for you in the cesspool as though that were the place to find you? Did you not want to leave because you thought if you looked hard enough, you would finally find you there? Would you give up that insanity please? You do not exist in the cesspool.

You keep looking for somebody who can give you an answer about what you need to be or do, and that's not really available. Do not ask about what you need to be and do. Ask what you need to choose. Ask the question and just sit with it.

What do I need to choose that would allow me to be everything I would like to be?

What do I need to choose that would allow me to be everything I desire to be?

The biggest mistake we see people making is they look at each of the parts of relationship as though studying the parts would give them clarity. Parts can't give us clarity. Only the whole can give us clarity. So instead of trying to figure out which parts are missing or what pieces are missing or what you should add or could add or should do differently or should have more clarity on, just allow the whole thing to be there and ask, "What choice can I make?"

If you will embrace the idea of moving beyond where anybody else is capable of living, you become an invitation for other people to step up to more of what they can be too. When you embrace this idea, there will also be some people who will go away from your life. They will leave and not want to have anything to do with you ever again. I lost many of my "best friends" when I started walking into this space. They just went away and didn't want to talk to me anymore because they didn't want me to change. They knew that if I changed, they would have no excuse for holding on to their own judgments about what was right and wrong in their universe, and that was too uncomfortable for them.

Tool: Choose in Ten Second Increments

Before reading this book, you didn't realize that there was the 990% that you could choose. It doesn't matter if you have chosen the 10% in this particular area your whole life; right now is a new 10 seconds.

Exercise: *You've got ten seconds to live the rest of your life, what do you choose? Beep! OK. That lifetime is over.*

You've got ten seconds to live the rest of your life, what do you choose? Beep! OK. That lifetime is over.

You've got ten seconds to live the rest of your life, what do you choose? Beep! OK. That lifetime is over.

You've got ten seconds to live the rest of your life, what do you choose? Beep! OK. That lifetime is over.

You've got ten seconds to live the rest of your life, what do you choose? Beep! OK. That lifetime is over.

Imagine what it would be like if your life were like that. Imagine that you can choose every ten seconds. Even if you have chosen the 10% because you thought that was the way life was or because you were trying to love your mom, hate your mom, love your dad, hate your dad, make them right or make them wrong or for any other reason, it doesn't matter. What if you realized: "Wow, this is a new ten seconds. I can make a totally different choice right now." And then what if you asked, "Am I choosing the 10% or the 990%?"

If you give up resisting and reacting to what you are choosing today and realize it is just a choice that you have available, you can choose something else with freedom. "Okay, I am choosing something else. What would I like to choose today?"

You always have choice. How much of your life are you creating based on "I have no choice?" Are you trying to find the *Lord of the Rings* choice, the one choice that will rule them all? This is a problem. People try to create one choice that will rule all other choices so that they will never have to make a different choice. The reality is you need to be able to make your choice in ten second increments. Choices that last forever are what create no choice in your life.

How many "forever" choices have you made that are destroying your current life? *Everything that is times a godzillion will you destroy and uncreate it all, please? Thank you. Right and wrong, good and bad, POD and POC, all nine, shorts, boys and beyonds.*

Most people ask, "What would I not like to choose today?" They live from resistance by asking, "What would I *not* like to show up today?" They think, "Oh no! I know this is going to show up today." They don't want it to show up and therefore it shows up.

What if there was nothing you needed to change? What if there was just the choice to change every ten seconds? Most people try to get to consistency, as though consistency will make their life predictable. Why would you want a life that was predictable, safe and boring?

What would be the value of having a consistent life? Do you want to know everything is consistent so you can control it? If you are not willing to see a different possibility, then you are trying to make your life consistent and boring. Do you think that is the way for you to fit in this reality? You are a humanoid and you can't fit in this reality. You can choose the 990% instead and generate something you have never been willing to generate—your own reality.

Needing Reference Points

To a certain extent you will go back to what's familiar, even if it's crappy, because that way you know where you are. You make a choice to go back to what you know because that is your reference point for your reality. Your reference points are the energies you consider your life to be, and if any of those energies go missing, you panic and go looking for them.

Let's say you've spent your whole life worrying about money, worrying about money, worrying about money. You consider that to be your life. Then something changes and your worry about money is gone. You wake up in the morning and you say, "Oh my god, something is missing! What's missing?" The worry is missing.

I used to suffer from back pain, and for about a year and a half I was flat on my back. I thought, "I can't stand this. I'm going to kill myself unless something shows up that gives me a different option." I couldn't lift a bag of groceries. I couldn't get out of the house. I just lay there and watched television. This was not a life. As a result of my demand for change, I met someone who did Rolfing, which is a kind of deep tissue massage. After five sessions of Rolfing, I was out of pain. I woke up one morning and I said, "There's something wrong. There's something wrong. What is it?" The pain was missing. I was out of pain for the first time in two and a half years.

In a circumstance like that, 90% of the time, you recreate the problem because that's what you have decided your life is. You will go looking for the problem and you will do whatever it is you know how to do to take you back to that place again rather than asking, "Who am I today? What else can I generate? What else might be possible now?" How about starting where you are, rather than going back to find the energy you called your life to see if you can step back into it?

If you actually go looking for what your point of view was before you changed it or for what you had before you changed your point of view, you will recreate the whole thing. This is one of our greatest talents and abilities. Dain and I call it recreating crap. What if we didn't do that?

You have a moment of choice when you become aware of what is creating your life the way it is. You can either go back into the cesspool or you can say, "No, I'm swimming in the clear pool now."

Some people want to change but they feel that they have to have their reference points to know what they are changing or even if they are changing. They have the opportunity to change and have an entirely different life but when they come right up to the edge of it, they turn around and go in the opposite direction. You look for your past reference points to show you that you have a reality. But what if you had no reality?

Have you misidentified and misapplied that if you don't buy into everybody else's reality you will be lost? Do you find that other people's reality is fun? Or would you rather die than live that way? What if you can change and have a reality that is different from what other people have? A lot of people live lives of what we call quiet desperation. Maybe it is just incredible boredom!

Do You Love Hating Your Life?

Do you love hating your life? "I love my life so much I won't give it up." This is like having a love-hate relationship with a lover. "I love my life but I hate it; I love my lover but I hate them so much I want to get rid of them and get a new one, but I can't because if

I lose this one I don't know if I will ever have another one." What? That's just nuts!

Are you bored? If you are being bored, you don't want to have fun. If you were having fun you would stop being bored. The truth is that you love being bored. It gives you all kinds of power over other people. It is also one of the ways you create the love you have for hating your life.

How do you change that? Look for something that nurtures your body and your soul and do that for at least an hour a day and one whole day each week. As soon as you have an awareness that one small moment is fun, be grateful for the fun that it is, enjoy the hell out of it and then ask, "Okay now, where is the next ten second increment of joy and fun?" Then start applying that to every aspect of your life.

You have to laugh at how incredibly ridiculously we are at creating our lives. Here we are saying, "I hate this" and yet we keep doing it over and over again. Doing the same thing over and over again and expecting a different result is called insanity! But we won't admit that we are insane because we are trying to prove that we are sane by choosing the same thing over and over again!

Are You Getting What You Deserve?

The word *deserve* means to *devote oneself to being of service.* Are you of service? Many people think it means to be worthy, and that you deserve in return for service. None of that is true.

"I got what I deserved" is an interesting point of view. No you didn't; you don't deserve anything. Do you deserve to breathe? Just because you are breathing doesn't mean you deserve to breathe. There are a lot of people in the world who are a waste of breath! You are an infinite being with infinite possibilities; you breathe from choosing, not from deserving. What if your life wasn't about what you deserved but what you were willing to choose and willing to receive?

If you make your life about what you deserve, it puts you in a constant state of judgment of you and everything in your life. There is no deserving. There's no reason and justification that means you deserve anything. You don't even deserve to breathe; it is simply a choice you have.

Why Did I Choose This?

"Why?" is not a good question. Asking *why* will lead you in circles and eventually you will end up back where you started. The reasons and decisions for choosing something are irrelevant if you're willing to choose something different now.

Choice is senior to process. You can make a choice or you can process and analyze yourself until the cows come home. Dain used to try to process everything to make a change. His basic point of view was, "I can't change this until I've processed it." One day I asked him, "Can you change your socks without processing?"

Dain said, "No, I don't process. I just change my socks."

I said, "Okay, you can just change your life too!"

Instead of asking *why* ask, "How does it get any better than this?"

Tool: How Does It Get Any Better Than This?

When you choose to say the words **"How does it get any better than this?"** you are literally asking for the vibration of how something gets better. This requires you to let go and allow the universe to show you how it gets better. You can't control it. All you can do is ask the universe for the favor of assistance and receive that assistance from wherever it may show up.

The more you ask the question **"How does it get any better than this?"** the more doors open. Things expand and everything becomes light and easy. That's being in the 990% of possibility. As soon as you say, "Well it can't get any better than this," you go back to the 10%. This occurs when you are going along and using the question **"How does it get any better than this?"** Everything's easy and then you say, "Wow, this has been going on too long. It's too good. Something's got to happen." Right there, you make a decision. You decide something's got to happen—so something happens. You have jumped yourself out of the clear pool and into the cesspool. It's okay. You can choose again and say, "Okay, I'm back in the cesspool. Never mind, I am going back to the clear pool."

Chapter Twelve

CHOICE CREATES AWARENESS

Ultimately the target here is to get to the point where choice is not about whether something is rewarding or not rewarding, it's not about whether it is good or bad. It's just a choice. When you make a choice, you are instantly more aware. Choice creates awareness; awareness does not create choice.

When you start to create from choice, all of a sudden a new universe begins to open up for you. You choose and then you get to see what that choice creates.

The problem is we act like we are the effect of every choice we make. This occurs because we were taught that we have to be aware of the consequences of our actions, which we can't control because we are not God. We were never taught to ask, "Okay, what is this choice going to generate or create in my life?" Have you ever made a choice that made absolutely no sense yet something extraordinary opened up from it? Choice is greater than anything else. Everything is a choice.

After I got divorced, I made a choice to have an affair with a woman who then told everybody that because I had chosen to have an affair with her, she was obviously the most conscious person in Access Consciousness. She told everyone who was doing classes with me at that time that she was now the Queen of Access. As a result, seventy-seven people left Access, which had a severe impact on my business.

I did not go into the wrongness of me. I said, "Okay, that was not my best choice!" I had made myself unaware so I could go ahead and do what I had decided I wanted to do, which was to have the affair. It had nothing to do with being in the question. I had the point of view that I was so conscious that I could get away with it even though I knew it was not a good idea. I didn't ask a question like, "Is this rewarding?" because I didn't really want to know the answer. I didn't really want to see what was going to happen. I just made the choice to have the affair.

As a result of that, I became aware of the amount of judgment that was functioning in the world. And because destruction showed up for me after making that choice, I discovered there was a point of destruction (POD) as well as a point of creation (POC) connected to a point of view. It explained the decisions that become destructive in our life and how we create destructive patterns. We now use POC and POD in the clearing statement because they eliminate the things we have created with our points of view.

Prior to this experience, I hadn't put a lot of attention on judgment, but because of it I realized that judgment is what people use to separate or to connect, and by seeing that there was a point of destruction, I became aware of how judgment is so destructive to our lives.

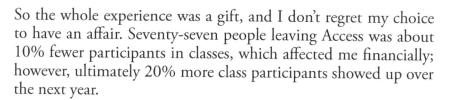

So the whole experience was a gift, and I don't regret my choice to have an affair. Seventy-seven people leaving Access was about 10% fewer participants in classes, which affected me financially; however, ultimately 20% more class participants showed up over the next year.

Every choice creates awareness. Your choice may not end up being something that turns out "well," but the awareness that can come from it can be huge!

Controlling Others with Your Choices

Unfortunately you are not God and you cannot control what other people will choose based on what you choose with regard to them. You have to acknowledge that and ask, "Will this choice be rewarding?" and "Will this choice be a contribution?" Even if you don't get a cognitive answer, asking these questions will open the door to awareness that you would not have been willing to have before.

Once I had the affair with this woman, I couldn't undo the damage she was going to do to other people's lives as a result of it. You cannot control what someone will do after you interact with them. They are going to take what you have said or done and run with their own insane worldview. They are not going to have the same point of view you do.

This is what you have to be aware of when you choose something with someone. Just because you see something that could be possible does not mean the other person will. You have to look at what they see as possible and not possible as well.

There Is No Good Reason for Anything

You cannot determine how the points of view that people function from were created because people make all kinds of weird decisions. You will not get anywhere looking for *where or why*. Just know that people make decisions and that is their choice.

I had a friend who was a songwriter. He had once been very successful but he had not had success for a long time. He wanted to work on his success and was asking what it would take to get it back. His wife had a lot of talent and ability too, and I worked with both of them. Nothing happened until one day when Dain was working with them. He asked the husband, "Would you be willing to be hugely successful again?"

The husband said, "Yes, absolutely."

Dain asked, "Even if it meant losing your wife?"

"Yes, absolutely, he replied.

His wife looked at him and said, "I just realized I've been holding you back all these years. I didn't want you to be any more successful because I thought you would leave me."

Dain asked her if she would be willing for her husband to be a success. She said yes. A year later she was diagnosed with a brain tumor, and she spent five years dying of brain tumors. Dain and I tried everything we could to get her to change her point of view about getting a brain tumor. She wouldn't do it. She died.

Once before the wife died, I went to Nashville to visit my friend. When I walked into the house I saw that the wife had redecorated the entire place so it would be a man's house not a woman's. She had done all this knowing full well that she was going to die. I asked her questions about choosing death instead of something else and finally she said, "I knew I had to get out of the way in order for him to be a success again."

She could have chosen to change, but she chose death over changing. Death was a perfect, preferable choice over change. There are a lot of people who have that point of view. Rather than change something, they would prefer to die.

It is bizarre that people would choose something like that, but they do. It is just a choice they make. There is no *why* they choose it—they just choose it.

You Can't Save People

You can't stop people from doing what they have decided to do. I once made the error of telling a friend that her relationship was a mistake. She had been through several failed relationships and she asked me to tell her when she was making a mistake with the men she picked. She found someone and came to me saying, "Oh, he's so perfect, he's so wonderful, he's the perfect man for me." That wasn't what I saw—and because she had asked me to tell her when she was making a mistake, I said, "He's a lunatic and he's going to beat you."

She was furious with me. "How can you say that? I can't believe you would say that to me!" She stopped talking to me. Three years later he was beating her. Two years after that she had a baby, and he started beating the baby. Then he went to church and became a good God-fearing Christian, so he prayed over them before he hit them. Out in public they would pray at every meal for God to bless them in what they were doing but he was still a lunatic. She stayed with him.

She has been with him for twenty-five years and he's still a lunatic. She has divorced every part of her in order to make that relationship work. It wasn't her brightest choice, but I wasn't bright either because I actually told her what she said she wanted me to tell her. I learned then that it is not wise to believe what people tell you. Be aware and tell people what they really want to hear. Never tell them what is true.

Tool: Tell People What They Can Hear

This is one of the greatest tools available to you in relationships. It will save you grief to a degree you can't begin to imagine. Have you ever tried to tell someone something that you thought they should know that they weren't actually willing to hear?

Who is the one who gets the grief as a result of it? It's always you! The other person will always make you wrong. They will always get pissed off at you and then you have to spend five hours explaining to them how it was not actually what you just said.

Be aware of what other people can receive. That's true kindness. Even if you're in a relationship with someone, keep what you know to yourself unless they ask you a question. They will not be willing to hear anything unless they want to know and they ask for that knowing. All you can do is contribute to the person; you cannot help them or make them more conscious.

If you want to help a friend by telling them how you see something or what you know about their situation, stop and ask yourself, "Have they asked a question about this and are they interested in this?"

My friend Mary was ninety-five years old when she suggested to me that I could have a better relationship with my wife if I stopped trying to tell her what she couldn't hear. Mary said it was a mistake to assume you must share everything with your mate. Big mistake. It doesn't contribute to the relationship at all. So I stopped telling my wife what she didn't want to know about or what she didn't want to hear and our relationship improved.

Mary said that she and her husband Bill would discuss things and then Bill would say, "Okay, Mary, the complaint department is now closed." That meant, "We will not talk about this subject anymore. This is not a subject we will ever agree on; therefore you cannot complain about the fact that I don't agree with you. This will not be a topic of discussion ever again."

Mary explained, "We agreed that we were never going to agree, so we just said, "Let's not discuss it anymore. It is so much easier when you know what you don't need to talk about!" She was into metaphysics and went to psychic healers all over the world. He believed you lived, loved, worked and died and that was it. She spent hundreds of thousands of dollars doing different things and she said, "Bill said that if that's what I needed to do then I should do it. And so I did." But she never tried to talk to him about these things.

This is a more sane way of having a relationship. Mary and Bill truly cared for each other and they contributed to each other. They were one of the few couples I know that had a great and phenomenal relationship. Their relationship wasn't based on sharing. It was based on the fact that each one of them supported the other in whatever their point of view was.

Let Me Share This with You

The way sharing works is this: You know that A, B, C is possible and you try to share this with someone who only knows X, Y, Z is possible. Unless the other person makes a choice for something different or at least has a question in their universe about what else might be possible, they will never see A, B, C, nor will they step into it. If you're making an effort to create a relationship and you're trying to share what you know is possible, you will cut off everything you know about A, B, C and try to start the relationship at X, Y, Z because you believe that then you will be able to get them to go to A, B, C.

One day Dain was jogging along the beach. He was full of energy, running with ease and enjoying his body because, for him, it is fun to run. A little way along the beach another guy came jogging the other way and was soon within 100 meters of Dain. At that moment, Dain felt like his body had no energy; he couldn't breathe, his lungs were filling up with fluid, and his coordination was all over the place. He kept running and asked, "What the hell is going on?" This happened with six other people as he was going along on the beach. They all had different body types and he was experiencing different things. Dain was really confused. He kept asking, "What is going on here?" and then he suddenly realized that his point of view was that he wanted to share with people what he knew to be possible with embodiment and how the body could be a source of joy. Every time he tried to share this awareness with them and their bodies energetically or any other way, he had to go down to their level.

This is the way sharing works energetically. If you are functioning from the desire to share a point of view, you must be willing to look at what the other person can receive because unfortunately, sharing is not what you think it is. What actually seems to be the case is that you have to diminish you because the other person has no desire to receive what you wish to share with them. We always assume when we find something great that other people would desire to share that and to have that greatness too. This is a mistake we all make. The reality is you have to look at the situation and ask, "Can the other person receive this? Do they desire to receive it?"

Sharing with the One You Love

When Dain started using Access Consciousness tools he went from wanting to kill himself to becoming happy and joyful. There was so much peace in his world he wanted to share it with his mom. He said, "My mom was one of the saddest people I knew, so I kept asking her, 'Would you like to come do this Access stuff? It is so cool! Will you check out some of this information? Do you want to do this class? Do you want to look at the website?'" She couldn't even hear it. She either never responded or she would say something like, "No I have this other thing to do." Dain's response was, "What are you talking about?"

One day I said to Dain, "Do you realize that your mother loves being sad and unhappy and she doesn't want to change?"

Dain finally realized that it actually made his mother happy to be that sad. He had desired to give her something she didn't want, which was the same as judging her to be inferior to him. He saw that in trying to get his mom to change, he was actually being unkind to her. He chose to POC and POD his point of view and he energetically said to his mom, "Mom, you know what? I am really sorry. I apologize. I have been a superior asshole trying

103

to give you what I think you should want. I am totally over that and I won't ever do it again. You can be sad, happy or whatever you want. I love you totally and completely just as you are." Two weeks later his mom called and asked, "Why don't you ever invite me to any Access classes?"

He had been inviting her for two and half years, but she couldn't hear it because Dain was vested in the outcome of wanting her to get something instead of being willing for her to be and do whatever worked for her.

Being Vested in the Outcome

If you are vested in the other person changing or in the other person getting something or in the other person sharing with you, they can't ever get it. You have to be in allowance of what they have chosen and know it is right for them. It is their choice, it is their life, and they have to live it the way they choose. When you get vested in wanting them to do something different, nothing will change.

When you get vested in someone changing, you suck yourself into their 10% and function from there. You buy into their viewpoints rather than being the space of the 990% that you can be. When you are willing to just be the way you know is possible, when you are not trying to change someone, you become the invitation and the inspiration for them to choose differently.

Are you refusing to be the inspiration you can be? How much of you are you diminishing so you won't inspire others to be greater? *Everything that is times a godzillion will you destroy and uncreate it all, please? Thank you. Right and wrong, good and bad, POD and POC, all nine, shorts, boys and beyonds.*

Just for Me

How often have you been able to share good news with your friends and have them be grateful for your success? Ninety percent of them will think, "Well, how come you got that and I didn't?" or "Well, of course you would get that, you asshole!"

Don't tell people about the things you do that are highly successful. This results in using others as a reference point, and if you use others as a reference point for your success, you inevitably pull yourself out of the 990% and perpetuate the 10% reality. You will keep going back to the 10% because that's the reference point for where you belong. It's operating in contextual reality: Where do I belong? Where do I fit?

You can't hold on to your past reference points—even when you are dealing with people you care about. You have to be willing to let people choose to go if they choose to go. You may say something like, "I can't let him go. He's been in my life for forty years!" If you're tempted to think like this, ask yourself if the person is truly a good friend. Just because you have known someone for forty years doesn't make them a good friend. Are they envious or jealous? That's not a good friend. Do they judge you? That's not a good friend. These are people you don't attempt to share things with.

You don't have to get rid of anybody, anyway; just start using their judgment as a way of getting them to give you what you want.

This is the way you have to live your life: "Just for me, just for fun, never tell anyone." And enjoy the hell out of your life.

Chapter Thirteen

CREATING A NEW RELATIONSHIP

Are you looking at your relationship and asking yourself, "How do I fix this?" Why would you try to fix something that doesn't work? It's not that it is broken; it just doesn't work. You may think that is what you're supposed to do, but it isn't true. If something doesn't work, don't try to fix it. Do something different.

You keep trying to take the thing that is never going to work and fix it to make it better or make it work rather than changing it. Doing relationship differently is not going to work. Relationship in this reality is set up to not work. You can't do something that is set up to not work, keep doing it the same way and act like it's going to work. How many times have you done the same thing over and over again, thinking you're going to get a different result? Did you know that that is one of the definitions of insanity?

Of course, you have never tried to fix a relationship that wasn't working, have you? Or have you tried to fix it nonstop? And since you couldn't fix it, did you decide the only person you could fix was you? Did you keep on changing, folding, stapling, mutilating, cutting off body parts and anything else you could think of to make it work—and it still didn't work? Or did you think, "It's sure to work when I find the right one, the true one, the real one?" Sorry. That's not going to work either. Please stop reading romance novels and look at what is going on. How about choosing awareness over romance?

It is not right or wrong to have a relationship; it's a choice. One should always have choice.

The purpose of a relationship should be to increase the survival and income of both people. You want to be more than just surviving—you want to be thriving! Thriving and abundance is the target, not just living together, not just functioning together. It's having somebody who will support you in growing as much as you can and having somebody you can support in growing as much as they can.

You will notice that this is a slightly different point of view about relationship than you see in the rest of the world. Doesn't it feel a lot lighter?

Once you start using these tools, you will be different. You will need to acknowledge that you are changing and opening doors to other possibilities. If you are in a relationship at the moment, your partner will either go through the doors with you, enjoy it and become more of who they are and more of the person you married, or they will decide they have to go away.

Tool: Destroy and Uncreate Your Relationships Every Day

What does it mean to destroy and uncreate your relationship? Well, let's say you have been fighting and you want to get your partner back into the bedroom. You could ask, "Do you want to get a divorce or would you like to create something different and let the past be gone?" If they say yes, you can destroy and uncreate the relationship and start over.

This is a tool you can use every day. When you wake up each morning, say to each other: **"Everything our relationship was yesterday I destroy and uncreate it all. Right and wrong, good and bad, POD and POC, all nine, shorts, boys and beyonds."**

Do this every morning.

This tool has been used successfully by many people. One lady asked her husband to do this on their anniversary. He had asked her, "What would you like for our 25th wedding anniversary?" and she said, "I would like us to destroy and uncreate our relationship every morning." He was shocked and asked, "What do you mean? Do you want to get a divorce?" She said, "No, I just want to destroy and uncreate everything our relationship was yesterday so we are starting new every day. Every day will be a new beginning, not based on any old points of view." She said their relationship has been working well for them for several years now.

This tool gives you a way to generate your life so it is always on a create cycle and not on a destruct or maintenance cycle. A lot of people try to maintain their relationships after they get them going. Why would you want to maintain them? Maintenance is boring. You want to get your relationships on a create cycle. When you destroy and uncreate your relationship with your mate, your kids or your business, you can generate something new.

It is a lot more fun to create your relationship like Adam Sandler and Drew Barrymore in the movie *50 First Dates*. This movie is about a woman who has a condition where she can't remember anything after she goes to sleep. Every morning when she wakes up, she has to start over again and she spends the first hour of her day learning what her life was like yesterday so that she can have an awareness of where she is today. She starts each day brand new with no judgments carried forward so, for her, every day is full of possibilities and adventure.

You can use this tool with your kids, parents, friends, boss, co-workers, employees and even your pets. You can destroy and uncreate your relationship with anyone you have a relationship with. If you do this every day, suddenly you will have a different kind of relationship with them. They will be able to talk to you about things they have never talked about before, and you will be able to talk with them about things you always wanted to and never did. This tool puts you in a constant state of generating or creating a relationship instead of functioning from the old point of view.

My youngest son used to be consistently forty-five minutes late for everything, and this used to drive me crazy. I would scream and rant and rave at him every time he showed up late.

He would call and say, "Hey, Dad, let's get together." I might have an hour and a half free, so I'd say yes, but he'd be an hour late so we'd only have half an hour together. He would ask, "How come you never stay?" and I would say, "Because I have a life and you don't, which is why you'll be late and not care about it. But I do!"

Finally my youngest daughter said, "Dad, why do you bother? It never changes anything."

I said, "You know what? That's a good point of view. I'm over my old viewpoint. I'll allow him to be late whenever he wants."

About two weeks after that, my son called and said, "Hey, can we have breakfast?"

I said, "Sure," knowing that I had forty-five minutes to do a couple of other things before I met him. When I got to the place we were meeting, he was standing on the corner tapping his foot, which is what I always used to do. He said, "Where have you been? I've been here for thirty minutes!"

Oops. I had destroyed and uncreated everything my relationship had been with him. I assumed he would be late because he was always late, but now he was no longer late. Since then he's been on time. How does it get any better than that?

When you destroy and uncreate your relationship, you get rid of all the key points of view you have decided about the relationship. You destroy all the judgments you have about who or what the other person is, who and what you are, who and what you are supposed to be, and who or what you can't be. That opens the door to something greater.

Exercise: What Would You Like as a Relationship?

If you truly wish to create a relationship, start by writing down a list of all the things you would like the person you are living with to have, and then write a list of all the things you would not like them to have.

Make sure to write both lists because unless you are clear in your own world about what you would like that person to have as well as what you would not like them to have, you will get someone who has everything you want *and* everything you *don't* want.

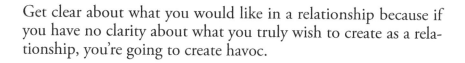

Get clear about what you would like in a relationship because if you have no clarity about what you truly wish to create as a relationship, you're going to create havoc.

Step One

Make two lists

* What would I like to have in my relationship?
* What would I not like to have in my relationship?

Don't ask for what you *want,* ask for what you *would like* in a relationship because that is different from what you want. I *want* always means I *lack.* You never want to ask for what you lack—because then you will get more of it.

If you look at the idea of two people increasing each other's capacity to thrive, you will become aware of the energy you would like to have as your life. Then you can see what another person might be able to contribute to that. The list is not about asking for a greater contextual reality where you win, lose, fit or benefit. The list is what you would like to have in another person you can contribute to. This is a totally different way of looking at relationship. It will allow you to be aware of the energy that a person is, which will allow you to start to receive that energy, instead of going, "Oh my God! Five foot eleven, blonde hair! I am so there!"

Write your list from non-contextual reality—from the possibilities, the choices, the questions and the contributions. Contextual reality would be: "I would like a man who has this amount of money or I would like a woman who has this body." You will get those things and then, more often than not, you will find that it is not enough. You will find you desire something greater because in the larger picture, this person is contributing to the energy of what you would like your life to be. The energy of what you would like your life to be is what needs to go on the list.

Ask for someone who will contribute to the constant expansion of every part of your life. Don't ask for someone who will support you—because you will end up with someone who's a complete jock strap or somebody who's nothing but a bra. That is not what you are looking for. You want somebody who will contribute to your life financially—or if you want the emotional upheaval, someone who will contribute emotionally, which means you are going to have lots of trauma and drama in your life.

Step Two

Destroy and uncreate all your decisions, judgments, conclusions and computations about how you can take care of yourself and do it all on your own. All of the "I can do it all by myself and I don't need anyone." *Everything that is times a godzillion will you destroy and uncreate it all, please? Thank you. Right and wrong, good and bad, POD and POC, all nine, shorts, boys and beyonds.*

The idea that you can do it all by yourself does not allow anybody to be in your life or to contribute to it. You can only have people in your life who would not be a contribution to you. You will have only people in your life who are needy and want you to take care of them.

The reality is that you can take care of yourself, but there is a difference between the decision "I can do it all on my own and I don't need anyone" and the awareness that you will be fine no matter what, even if you are alone. One is an awareness that does not exclude receiving contribution and the other is a decision that will cut off anybody who would contribute to your life. A decision like that will send away anybody who would like to contribute to your life because you can do it all on your own. Oops!

Step Three

Go over the list and ask, "Would this point of view be contractive or expansive?" Ultimately you're looking for a relationship that's expansive, not contractive. Contractive relationships are the ones where you divorce yourself. POC and POD everything that seems contractive and then leave yourself with all the things that have expansion in them. When you POC and POD all those contractive things, you won't be magnetically attracted to that energy anymore.

Look at the list of the items you don't desire in a relationship. Those will be all the things you have chosen consistently throughout all your relationships. If you become aware of these, you will divorce yourself less in your next relationship.

Is your list really long? Are you trying to eliminate a lot of people? Does that limit what can show up? Yes. It does. So look at your list and ask, "Is having this on my list creating a huge limitation?" If it is, then change it.

Tool: Make a Demand

You are the only power source that can keep you stuck where you are. You have all the answers to make sure that you never become greater than you are in this moment. To change it requires more than choice; you have to be willing to make a demand.

I got to a certain point in my life where I said, "You know what, this is just not enough. If this is all there is, I'm outta here. I'm dying. I'm not willing to live like this anymore." I made the demand that something greater would show up in my life or I was going to quit. I made that demand and within three weeks my life started to turn around.

A demand is what you make when you are out of answers and in the place of "This isn't good enough for me. I don't care what it takes, I don't care what it looks like, I don't care if I lose my life, I don't care who vilifies me, I don't care what happens. This has to change." That's the place you have to go, because requesting it, asking for it or wishing for it is not going to do it. If wishes were horses, beggars would ride. You have to make the demand of yourself, not of anybody else.

You could wait until you hate your life or you can make a demand now. "I'm going to create a life nobody else has. I don't care what it takes. I don't care what I have to do, who I have to do, who I have to be, whatever it is, I'm going to have a different reality and a different life."

Chapter Fourteen

CHOOSING A DIFFERENT KIND OF RELATIONSHIP

Contextual Reality

When you are functioning from contextual reality, you are always trying to assess the benefit of what you are choosing. You are constantly measuring and calculating to find where you fit, how you fit, that you fit or that you don't fit. You become consumed with working out how you can win or how you can avoid losing in any situation. How much energy does that take? A lot!

You have to judge everything and everyone constantly! Do I fit? Do I not fit? Do I benefit? Do I not benefit? Do I win? Do I lose? How can I avoid losing? Everything is about compare, contrast and judge. Where is the freedom in that?

Dain says, "It is tough to walk when your head is so far up your ass you need a glass stomach to see where you are going. I was really good at this, and it was interesting to see Gary, who knew he didn't fit. He had much more ease in his life because he was willing to know that he didn't fit. Gary didn't try to bend, fold, staple and mutilate himself, and seeing that made me realize, 'Okay, I am making this way more difficult than it has to be.'"

Are you making your life way more difficult than it has to be? Would you like to give up overcoming the obstacles in life to prove that you are a powerful being?

When you try to fit in, you have to bend, fold, staple and mutilate yourself out of existence, and the trouble is that as a humanoid, you have never been able to truly fit anywhere. You have probably tried desperately to fit in about eight godzillion times but no matter what you do, no matter how much you staple, fold and mutilate yourself, no matter how much you try to be like others, you still are not like other people, are you?

A humanoid can still function from contextual reality and many humanoids refuse to give it up because they figure eventually they're going to get it right. That's where they sabotage themselves. They believe they will get it right and they work hard to prove it. They keep thinking, "If I just get it right then I'll win, I will benefit, I will fit and I won't be a loser anymore."

The aim here is to get you out of trying to figure out how you fit, how you benefit, how you win or how you avoid losing (which is not the same thing as winning) and get you into the place where you can actually choose. There is no choice in the things you do that are about fitting, benefiting, winning or losing. There is only judgment. And judgment is always a nail in your coffin.

Non-Contextual Reality

Most people do business from the point of view of "What am I going to get? How am I going to win? How am I going to avoid losing? How am I going to benefit from this? Where do I fit in the scheme of things so I always win?" That's the same place people do relationship from.

In non-contextual reality, everything is about doing your life from possibilities, choice, question and the contribution you can be and receive. The great relationships we have known all have these elements in them. They ask, "What's possible? What choices do we have today? What do you want to do, honey? Do you want to do this or do you want to do something else? How can I contribute to making your life better?" There is no "I want." These relationships are always about contributing to the whole as well as to the individual. That is a very different place to run a relationship from.

When you do contextual reality as the source for your relationship, everything is about "Am I going to win? Am I going to lose? Am I going to fit? Am I going to benefit?" There's no question in any of it; there is only judgment.

When someone is doing sex from contextual reality, they have no choice but to try to control you, own you and keep you. They figure they will lose if you go away. If you do sex from the non-contextual reality, you say, "Thanks, that was fun. What else is possible?" Question. Choice. Do you want to go there again? Maybe.

A non-contextual relationship starts with always being in the question and never being in conclusion. Can you have that with somebody who's doing contextual reality? No. You would have to

117

have a contextual relationship with them unless they were asking for something different.

When you choose to have a non-contextual relationship, you start with questions: "What's possible with this person? What's possible for me with this person?" That requires you to be bluntly honest with yourself and ask, "What do I truly desire in a relationship?"

Shouldn't you actually have what you would like to have, no matter what it is? What if there was nothing wrong with desiring to have anything? Even if it seems insane to another person, who cares? It is your life, not theirs. You're not going to be happy having the relationship someone else desires. Why would you try to fit yourself into the relationship they want rather than actually looking at what you desire so you can create it?

Some people in relationship just want somebody to want them and to think that they are beautiful. That's it. There's no problem if that is what you would like to have, but you have to be aware of it so you won't bring somebody into your life who wants something completely different.

My first wife always wanted everyone to desire her. That was the only thing she wanted out of a relationship. Then as soon as you were willing to desire her, she didn't want you anymore. The relationship was over the day I committed to desiring her. The other thing she really liked was getting married. She didn't like *being* married, just *getting* married. The dress and the party was the part she liked best, so she got married five times.

I was number three. I married her because she was pregnant and I felt obligated to make sure my son was not going to be born as a bastard. I tried to make her life perfect and she tried to make my life hell. She wanted me to go away so then she could long for me. I was a moralist and a romantic, although I have since given those things up because I realized they actually don't serve in the long run.

I don't hate my ex-wives. I love them. I just can't live with them. Sometimes you love people you can't live with. It's not that you have to hate someone in order to leave them. You don't have to hate people to go away. You have to recognize that there are some people you can't live with no matter how much you love them. Do you love your parents—but you couldn't live with them for love nor money? After a certain point, you say, "I've got to have my own space and my own stuff." That's the thing I see. People divorce themselves to stay with somebody rather than realizing, "This isn't working. What can I do different?"

I don't want people to get a divorce based on the fact that they hate one another. I see how that animosity destroys their children, destroys their money flows, destroys everything. They're living from the lie that they hate the other person. Could an infinite being truly hate anyone? No. Why the hell are you trying to make yourself hate this person? It's not necessary. You simply have to recognize that loving somebody doesn't mean you can live with them.

If you want to create a non-contextual relationship, start by asking questions: What is possible with this person? What do I desire from a relationship? Can this person contribute to my life?

Playing with Possibilities

When Dain and I talk about contextual and non-contextual reality, we say that non-contextual reality is about greater possibilities. Sometimes when people hear this they say, "I've got to eliminate contextual reality from my life." No. Oneness and consciousness include everything without judgment, so contextual reality can exist, non-contextual reality can exist, and you can play in any field you wish. But you have to be in the play of it.

119

We tend to believe that when we get rid of the wrongness, everything will be right. That doesn't work, because you spend your entire life looking for the wrongness so you can figure out how to finally get right. As long as you focus on wrongness, what are you going to find? Wrongness!

The No Choice Choice

If someone else tells you that you have no choice, you will force yourself to have a choice. If you tell yourself that you have no choice, you absolutely have no choice.

For example, if someone tells you that you have no choice but to get married, you will usually say, "You can't tell me I have to get married!" That puts you in a constant state of conflict with yourself because on one hand you would like to get married, and on the other hand, you have been told you can't choose not to get married. So in order to prove the person who said you have no choice wrong, you have to keep doing what you're doing (not getting married) while assuming that you have no choice but to get married and trying to prove that it is not what you want because you were told you couldn't not choose it. How cool is that? Now you can maintain your 10% with ease. This is how we all maintain the 10% universe.

How many conflictual universes, paradigms and realities do you have to make sure that you stay in the 10% and never the 990%? *Everything that is times a godzillion will you destroy and uncreate it all, please? Thank you. Right and wrong, good and bad, POD and POC, all nine, shorts, boys and beyonds.*

You ask, "How do I change it?" Just change it.

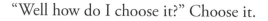

"Well how do I choose it?" Choose it.

"But what does it take?" Choosing it.

"But how do I do that?" Choose it.

Until you are willing to have true choice in your universe, the ease of choice can't show up for you. This is one of those things that can feel like shoving your head into a brick wall, but if you will get this, it can change everything.

Infinite Choice

Most of us don't know what choosing for us is. We try to choose for us, but we don't know how to do it. How can we know if we are choosing for us? How often do we question our choices? "Did I make a mistake? Did I make the right choice?" That is judgment. It is not awareness nor is it choice.

For the majority of our lives we have chosen against somebody else as though that was choosing for us. When you choose for you, it is never in relationship to anybody else or anybody else's point of view. It is simply about "Would I like to choose this?" It's not about whether anybody else would approve of your choice, think you were smart, notice what you chose or like you for it. Choice is: "I'm choosing this, and there's no reason for it."

At one time I worked in an antique shop, rearranging their furniture displays. They were so pleased with me that they told me I could put anything in the shop on layaway for as long as I needed to in order to buy it.

I said, "Wow, I can have anything in here?" Suddenly all of the things I really wanted and thought were so beautiful, I no longer cared about. I realized my point of view was that if I couldn't afford something, then it must be worth having so I should want to own it. How many of us pick our relationships that way? We pick what we "can't afford" because it must be valuable.

Become aware of when you say, "I chose this because…" The moment you say because you are justifying why you did whatever you did, which means you were not choosing for you. As soon as you go to justification or reason, you are choosing so somebody else will approve. That is not a real choice. When you choose from that place, who do you have to judge the most for being right or wrong? You! That is divorcing you in order to prove that you made the right choice.

In contextual reality, you try to get to perfect awareness so you can make all the right choices. It is not possible because choice creates awareness, awareness does not create choice. In non-contextual reality you can choose things and a moment later say, "Okay, I'm over that. What choice do I have now?" A choice is only good for ten seconds, so you can always choose again.

In non-contextual reality you can choose something and then say, "You know what? That did not turn out the way I hoped. Okay, never mind. Choose again." Choose again, choose again, and choose again. We tend to want to do the *Lord of the Rings* choice; we want "one choice to rule them all," which is really no choice. It is looking for an answer or a conclusion so that no more choices are required.

Seeking a set of answers is like functioning from the idea that if you get the right set of plug-ins on the power strip, when you hit the switch, your life will light up and start working the way you want it to. It doesn't happen because you are not allowing the universe to contribute to you. The universe is an abundant place that wants to gift to you all the time, and you refuse the gifts because they don't fit on your power strip!

The Either/Or Universe

Consciousness is a smorgasbord where you can have everything. The either/or universe is where you can only have this or that. Stop going to the either/or universe. Look at what is occurring and say: "Okay, I've got this. Now what else would I like to add to my life that would be fun too?" Do you think you are a limited being that can't do twenty-five things at once? We tend to function in life as though we have either this or that to choose from; we function as though there is limited choice. The truth is there are no limited choices.

Let's say you agree to go on a date, then something changes and you would prefer not to go. You don't want to say no in case you don't get asked again, but you can say, "I'm sorry, this doesn't work for me. What else is possible?" You make it wrong that you are choosing something different instead of asking, "What can I do to make this work?" It may seem like this is an either/or choice, but when you function from non-contextual reality you can have a different possibility.

Non-contextual reality is where you ask, "What are the possibilities here? What choices do I have? What questions can I ask? What contribution can I be and receive here?" Even if you have an appointment with somebody and they want you to be there at a certain time, you can say, "I'm sorry I'm not available then. I'd love to do it then, but I'm not available at that time. Is there another time we can do this?" Keep asking questions and more possibilities will show up.

What is this? What do I do with it? Can I change it? How do I change it? Those four questions will allow all of the angst about limited choice to go away and the either/or universe will cease to exist.

Tool: What Would It Take for This Relationship to Work for Me?

Look at what you want to create as a relationship. If you're already in a relationship, ask, "Is this relationship working for me now?" If the answer is yes, ask, "How do I generate it into something greater?" If the answer is *no,* ask, "What are the things I would like to have different to make it work for me?"

My second wife and I went to therapy and tried to get our relationship back together until finally I asked, "What would it take for this relationship to work for me?" Humanoids always want to make things work for the other person and they never consider themselves. That's what I had been doing. I was operating from the point of view of "How do I make the relationship work for her?" When I asked what it would take for the relationship to work for me, I came up with a list of eight things. I saw that seven of them were things my wife would consider as an attack on her basic being, so to ask her to change those things would be cruel. I knew I couldn't do that, so asked, "What's the least cruel choice?" I realized I would have to get a divorce. My wife thought I was a shit for getting a divorce, but I knew there was no way in hell I would get her to change those things.

Look at the things that don't work for you in your relationship and see which ones the person could actually change and which, if you asked them to change, would be like asking the leopard to change his spots. If there are more than five things that can't be changed, your relationship is probably never going to work for you. Please don't tell the other person what those things are. This is a way for you to gain awareness about what doesn't work for you. It is not a way to judge your partner.

Once you get that these are things that will never work for you in a relationship, ask, "Can I change this? How do I change this?

What can I do or be that will change this?" That will start to give you clarity about the areas you wish to be different in your relationship and then you can find ways to deal with it that are easier for you.

Don't Ask the Other Person to Change

When you ask the other person to change for you, they will always say, "Yes!" and then three weeks later, they will go back to what they were doing and be pissed at you for asking them to change. Asking somebody to change is not a good idea. Instead ask yourself, "Can I live with these things or do I need to see if I can get them to change this?"

If something doesn't work in your relationship, you will just feel irritated about those things. One of the items on my list of eight things that didn't work in my relationship with my ex-wife was that she had control over the money. She would overdraw the checking account every week and was continually bouncing checks. She would not agree to my being in charge of the checkbook. I was actually getting an ulcer because I feared we were going to run out of money. And of course, we were always out of money. When I did this exercise, I realized that for the relationship to work for me, I would have to be in control of the money and I knew that there was no way in hell she was going to let me have that. She wanted total control over everything. I was happy for her to be controlling but I was not interested in being on the edge financially any more.

Chapter Fifteen

HOW DO YOU KNOW
IT'S TIME TO LEAVE?

There are people who have begun using Access Consciousness tools in their lives and their husband or wife has not been interested in joining in. How do you keep your relationship when your partner is not interested in what you are doing?

As you use these tools, you will have more and more allowance of your partner's choices and points of view. If your partner is happy about you using Access Consciousness tools and is pleased you are enjoying yourself, then, great!

However, it can be that your partner will get upset with you because you are no longer doing the 10% and you are no longer controllable. You will know that is happening because they will use those five little words that strike terror to your heart, "Darling, we need to talk."

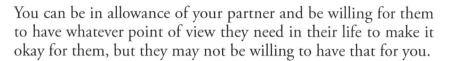

You can be in allowance of your partner and be willing for them to have whatever point of view they need in their life to make it okay for them, but they may not be willing to have that for you.

It may be that you are never going to get it right for them, and the relationship will never be the way you want it to be. If this shows up, you will need to ask a few more questions. You can ask, "What would it take for this marriage to work for me?"

Don't try to come to conclusion here because it is not about whether you have to leave your relationship. That's not the point. What has to happen is that you have to get you back. Once you get you back, if your partner needs you to be different than you are, then they will be the one who leaves.

Feeling Guilty About Leaving

Most humanoids won't leave their partner; they will get their partner to leave them. That is the humanoid way. You always have the point of view, "Well, I can handle it. I know that I'll be okay, but if I tell them they have to leave, they are going to feel terrible." You as a humanoid always know that you can leave, or they can leave you, and you will be fine. So you will always set it up so that they will leave you rather than you leaving them. It is a humanoid trait.

Do you feel guilty for feeling good about being out of your relationship? Are you actually feeling guilty—or are you trying to prove that you really care? A humanoid will always do that. They think, "I care for you and I feel guilty for leaving you, even though I was not really having much fun. I don't want you to know that my life is a lot better without you because that would devastate you."

So ask yourself how many years beyond the end of the relationship do you wish to stay? Two? Five? Ten? Twenty-five?

I worked with a lady who was hysterical about her marriage break up. She said, "I have been married for sixteen years and my husband left me. It is just so terrible and awful. I'll never recover!" I listened to this and I thought, "That's weird, she's saying all of this stuff but it doesn't have an ounce of energy on it." I said, "Truth, when did you leave him? When did you know it wasn't going to work? Six months before the marriage or six months after?"

She paused and looked at it and then she said, "Six months before."

I asked, "And you got married for what reason?"

She replied, "Well, we had already sent out the invitations."

So for $450 worth of invitations this woman had suffered for sixteen years.

Manipulating a Change

There is manipulation that is done to gain control over someone and there is manipulation that is done as a way of opening a possibility and a door. Most people try to do manipulation from the point of view of control, but you can also do manipulation as an invitation. If you do manipulation as an invitation, you can have anyone you want, when you want them. Recognize that you can't tell someone what they can't hear. Be willing to manipulate from total awareness and total presence.

This is a manipulation: "I realize how much I care for you and the one thing I want the most in life is for you to be happy. I realize I've done damage to you over the years, so what can I do to make up for the damage I've done?" The person will then have to decide what will erase the damage that's been done in the past.

Do not say, "I love you." Love equals obligation. "I love you" means now the other person is obligated to say it back to you.

You can say something like, "I realize I have given up so many parts and pieces of me over the years and I know I've suppressed you too. What would it be like if we actually liked each other and had fun together? Would that be a relationship you were interested in? That's the relationship I'm interested in. I would like every year we are together to be more wonderful than the last. Would that be of interest to you?"

Leave them with a question then it is their choice to go there or not.

If their commitment is, "Yes, I'd like to have a more wonderful life too" then you can ask, "Okay, so what would that look like for you? What can I do to facilitate that for you?" Keep asking what you can facilitate for them, and don't ask them for anything until they say, "What can I do for you?" It doesn't mean you have to give anything up!

Dying to Get out of a Relationship

Sometimes people have the point of view that the only way to have the life and the relationship they would really like is to die. The grand reset switch. Start again. The point of view is, "I can't

129

get out of this situation, I can't change it, I can't move it, I might as well die. It will be different next time." Dying is one of those choices that ends a lot of shit in your life. If you have this as your point of view, you will literally kill your body as a way to avoid having to choose for you.

I worked with a seventy-four-year-old lady in New Zealand who had developed cancer. I asked her, "What are you dying to get out of?"

She replied, "My relationship."

I asked, "Have you ever considered divorce?"

She said, "Oh, I could never do that; the children would never understand."

I asked, "How old is your youngest child?"

"Fifty-three."

I said, "Don't you think they'd rather have their mother divorced than dead?"

She replied, "Oh no, that would destroy their marriages."

So I said, "Okay. You know what, take your money and go home because I can't help you. If you are dying to get out of your relationship and you are physically dying and you are not willing to get a divorce, you have given yourself no choice. You are going to die."

And she did. Four months later she was dead. She was dying to get out of her relationship. It was not her only choice or her best choice, but it was the choice she made.

Are you dying to get out of your relationship? *Everything you have decided you are dying to get out of will you destroy and uncreate it all, please? Yes? Thank you. Right and wrong, good and bad, POD and POC, all nine, shorts, boys and beyonds.*

Staying Together for the Children

It is amazing how many people get married and then have a child to keep the marriage together, believing that having a child will somehow make the relationship better. And then they have another child to keep the first kid company, as if kids are just little bundles of joy and add no stress to the relationship.

Twenty years later they ask, "What just happened to my life?"

The truth is that children don't bring their parents together in order to be born to them in particular; they get them together for the genetic material. They usually don't care if their parents stay together and in fact are happy for them to not be together. Oftentimes kids would rather have them be apart so they can instill guilt in both parents and manipulate them more easily. And they know just how to do it!

When my second wife and I were about to get divorced, she wanted us to talk about it with our daughters. I brought the girls in and said, "Mom and I are going to get divorced." I watched the girls' universes expand with relief, and then they looked over at their mother, who was crying hysterically. The girls immediately went into their Mom's universe and contracted again. They knew their mother was not going to be happy if they were okay with the divorce because she had decided they should be upset about it. They pretended to be concerned, but they were actually empowered by our choice for divorce. It gave them the awareness that they didn't have to stick to something that wasn't working. Later they said, "I'm amazed you stayed as long as you did, Dad."

The girls now have a different kind of relationship with their friends and all the people in their lives as a result of our divorce. You can give your kids this freedom by the example you create, not by being "responsible" for them.

Your Responsibility to Your Children

What does *responsibility* really mean? First of all, you assume you have a responsibility to raise your children. Are you sure of that? Or is that what you have been told? How much have your children taught you? Maybe we have it backwards. Are you responsible for bringing them up—or are they responsible for bringing you up? Who is leading whom?

I worked with a man whose son had died at the age of nine. The boy was handicapped. He couldn't walk, talk or do anything when he passed away, yet the father acknowledges that his son taught him everything he knows about life.

What if parents of handicapped kids didn't see themselves as responsible for their kids? What if handicapped kids come in to the world to teach us and give us awareness of things we are trying desperately to not be aware of? Then once that occurs, they choose to leave because they don't need to be here anymore. It is amazing that there are beings who will do this kind of thing for us; it is truly a gift and a miracle.

Getting Divorced

The funny part about being a humanoid married to a human is that you always give them more in a divorce. Do you know why? Because you always know you can make it and you are never sure whether they can. You want to make it easier on them.

You will get what you want in a divorce if you are clear about what you want. But if you are trying to be fair and equitable, you won't get what you want. Fair and equitable in the court system means the man has to pay nothing and the woman gets nothing. How is that working for you?

Are you trying to create a divorce settlement that is fair and equitable? Fair and equitable is a judgment and each person sees what "fair" is differently. People have their own definition of fairness, which may not match anybody else's, and 99% of the time it doesn't.

Don't try to create a settlement that is fair and equitable. Create a settlement that will give you the most freedom in life.

A lady who was getting a divorce called me. She wanted my advice on how to make it easy. She said, "What do I do? We've got all this stuff."

I asked her, "Which one of you has the most money?"

She said, "I do."

I told her, "Pay off all debts. I guarantee you that if he takes half the debts, he is not going to pay them off. So you might as well pay off the debts and start creating your life."

If you were being fair and equitable, you would look at what is and ask questions to give you the awareness of what is possible. "Which one of us has the potential for creating the greatest future? Which one of us has the potential for creating the greatest amount of money? Which one of us has the willingness to generate a life?"

Fair is a judgment. If you want to be fair with somebody, that means what? Does it mean you don't want to treat them badly? You don't want to be harsh with them? Or does it mean you don't want to be wrong?

133

I knew a lady who got a "fair and equitable" settlement where her husband was supposed to pay child support of $400 per month for each of their three children. He decided it wasn't fair and equitable to him and he wasn't going to pay it. His viewpoint of fair and equitable was that she took the children, she paid for the children and he got to see them when he wanted to. He was more willing to go to jail than he was to pay child support. In the process, he ended up losing his job and all his money. Finally he was able to get a job where he earned just enough to survive but not enough to pay his child support. He went through all that to prove his point of view of what was fair and equitable.

You always have to create judgment in order to figure out whether you are being fair. Fair and equitable are about satisfying the other person's judgment. What actually is fair and equitable has nothing to do with it.

A man I know got divorced and gave his wife $4000 a month for fourteen years and close to $1000 a month for ten years thereafter. He gave her all the assets and he took all the debts. The wife complained that he took the best years of her life and then threw her away. She spewed vitriol about her ex-husband to every person she could get to listen to her. Was that fair and equitable or was that just her point of view? That was just her point of view.

The Fallback Position

A fallback position is the position you fall back to when you don't want to go forward, even when you know you could. It is the perfect reason and justification for holding on to a limitation because, in your world, you are the only one who has this reason and justification and it's one that nobody else would ever understand.

Dain explains it like this: "I grew up in a ghetto in the worst part of Los Angeles. There were three colors there. There was black, there was brown and there was me! I was the only white kid for eight miles around! When I'd work with Gary, everytime he would come up against something I didn't want to deal with or I didn't want to choose, I'd say, "You don't know where I grew up!" as though that was a reason and justification.

"You don't know where I grew up! You don't know what happened to me as a kid! If you had lived my life, you would not talk about choosing other possibilities!" I would usually say it in my head, but one day I finally made the mistake of saying it out loud. I said, "You know what? If you had grown up in the ghetto, you would have problems like this too!" As soon as I heard myself say it, I realized how utterly ridiculous it sounded. I was arguing for my own limitations and holding them in place with the perfect reason and justification! That was not bright. I asked Gary, "Will you help me through this?"

He said, "Okay. Would you be willing to give that up as your fallback position?"

What are you using as the excuse and justification for not having the relationship and the life you say you desire? How many fallback positions do you have so you don't have to go forward with your life? *Everything that is, times a godzillion, will you destroy and uncreate it all, please? Thank you. Right and wrong, good and bad, POD and POC, all nine, shorts, boys and beyonds.*

Writing People out of Your Life

Are you struggling with the need to be part of human reality and to function with others when you would rather be like the Tibetan monks who just head off into a cave, divest themselves of everything and live in bliss?

It is true that the monks live in bliss in their caves—but only until they come out of the cave. Then they're buried in shit because they have no tools to deal with life. With these Access tools you can have that kind of bliss and at the same time be unaffected by whatever somebody else might choose. When you are willing to be all of you, you realize you don't have to exclude anything from your life.

Do you try to find that blissful space by writing people out of your life continuously? Do you always manage to find a reason to judge every friend you have so you can leave them?

The truth is that it's possible to have the space of being the joy, the gratitude, the connection and the communion with all things and to have a greater connection with all the people in your life even if they are not choosing that joy for themselves. This is how allowance works.

Oneness and consciousness include everything without judgment. So nothing has to be eliminated from your life. Everything has to be added to your life.

This way of being actually gives you a greater connection with others. It allows you to be more present with people and to be there for them for whatever they're willing to have and for whatever they desire or require without feeling like it is diminishing or taking away from you. You find that you can live with other people no matter what they choose and they don't affect you in the same way they did before.

When you discover non-contextual reality and what that can generate for you, you may take the point of view that non-contextual reality is the greater choice than contextual reality. You may begin to think you have to eliminate people from your life who primarily choose contextual reality. That makes you contract again because you usually don't want to eliminate these people from your life—and you don't have to. If the people around you are choosing contextual reality, you don't have to eliminate them from your life at all. You can choose whatever you choose, and all the other people in your life can choose whatever they choose; you just don't have to be the effect of it anymore.

How do you deal with a friend who does a lot of contextual reality? You tell them, "I love you no matter how crazy you are" or "I don't care how crazy you are, I still love you." They will appreciate it and will usually say, "Thanks!" They know they are being crazy and that doing crazy shit is not serving them, and your acknowledgement relieves the pressure of their judgment of themselves. It also relieves you from being vested in the outcome of them changing and it eliminates your judgment of their choices.

Some of your friends will walk away from your life when you adopt this way of being. Others will look and say, "Ooh, that looks like more fun" and they will start changing too. Some will perceive the space of allowance you are being but not change anything in their lives. Some will get angry and destroy their relationship with you. It's their choice. It's not that you are choosing to divorce them; they are choosing to divorce you.

Do you do whatever it takes so people will not get upset and divorce you? Do you contract down and squeeze yourself into whatever is necessary so they won't divorce you? What if you could be in allowance of them and say, "If you feel you have to do that, okay. I still care about you every bit as much as I did and I won't ever stop." That would be a divorceless relationship.

A divorceless relationship expands your world and theirs. It doesn't contract it. As humanoids, we spend so much of our time trying to eliminate things from our lives. We are always looking for what is wrong so we can eliminate the wrongness and then the rightness will show up. Do you do this? How is that working for you? What if there was no right and no wrong? What if everything was available to you? What could you choose that you're not choosing now?

Keep Choosing 990%

Once you move into the space of the 990%, you start to realize how much bigger life is and your world expands. Things start to happen for you and you see that if you had maintained the 10%, that opportunity would never have shown up in your life. You would never have experienced the 990%. You begin to realize that everything you ever desired in your life is available to you *if* you go for the 990%. It is not always comfortable but even in discomfort you will ask yourself, "Would I rather be in the cesspool—or would I rather be uncomfortable out here in the ocean of possibilities?"

When you realize you can choose this all the time, you begin to invite others to play with you. Life goes out of the serious and into the play. It goes from being intense into the absolute joy of possibilities. And when things come along that in the past might have dragged you down or caused you to respond from the 10%, you wonder why those things even bothered you. Keep choosing the 990% and life gets easier and easier. The more you choose the 990%, the more you realize there are different choices available.

In the realm of relationship, you will choose a partner who is in contextual reality so dynamically that you have to go there in order to have sex and copulation. When you are willing to say, "Even if this great sex goes away, I'm not divorcing me this time," you will have choice. In actual fact, you will not be losing anything. You will be adding more to your life. You don't have to cut things out of your life to function from this space of 990%. You don't have to cut anything out of your life. But you do have to be aware, so you don't get sucked back in.

You can have everything and everyone in your life, and with each person in each situation you have choice. You can choose how you are going to interact with each individual. Do you desire to go out and have sex? That may not be your choice. But because that's not the choice, it doesn't mean you can't have a connection, closeness and friendship with that person.

Dain says, "Before I knew I could choose this other way of being, my choices were mount it, kill it or leave it. That's what I thought my options were. Now I can say, 'Hi, how are you?' and there's another world of possibility available because I am aware that I have choice. Part of having that choice is the recognition that I don't have to leave anybody in order to have my life. And if they choose to leave, that's okay; I don't have to have someone else to have my life."

You can create the illusion of relationship if that is what someone desires. You don't have to buy it as true. You can be whatever you need to be for them, and it doesn't mean you have to change you at all. You can be the parent your children need and still be you, you can be the boss your employees need and still be you and you can be the lover your partner needs and still be you.

Choosing Change

Have you decided you are the one person who cannot overcome your own objection? When you say, "I'm not changing this," no one, including you, will ever make you change it. You are the only one who can ever change anything in your life and it is your choice whether you do or not. It is true that if you change, you will lose the reality you currently have. But is this reality good enough?

Just decide to change. As soon as you make the choice to change, change has occurred. You may assume the only way you know something has changed is if you feel different. No. Feeling different does not mean change has occurred. You change all the time and it doesn't involve a feeling of any kind. It's not about feeling the change; you are the change. You don't have to do something; you just have to decide to change. How will you know you have changed? You will know you have changed when things start to show up differently for you.

Chapter Sixteen

WHAT ARE YOU ATTRACTED TO?

The law of attraction is the idea that whatever you think about, you're going to attract. Is the law of attraction real? Does it work? No. People believe the law of attraction will generate an improvement in their lives, but if you are doing the law of attraction, what is your point of view? Your viewpoint is that you are not—or do not have—what you are asking for. It's that you need something brought in from outside of you because you are missing something.

Plus you already have all underlying points of view that don't allow it.

It is important to realize that your point of view creates your reality; reality does not create your point of view. When you have the point of view that you have to attract something to you so you can be it or have it, it means that you have to make sure that you are not the thing you are trying to attract. This is the chink in the armor of the law of attraction. This is why the law of attraction, instead of creating expansion, creates a contraction. Even when you attempt to attract a larger life, you will attract to you those things that create a smaller life.

Isn't it amazing how brilliant we are at creating the most convoluted methods to control and diminish our lives? This is one of the ways you make sure you never get to be more than 10% of you.

Have you ever noticed that you are attracted to people who are less than you? Why is it that somebody who is less than you is attractive to you, but somebody who is more than you is not attractive?

You are trying to feel like you belong. You are heading towards the belonging of a small life that doesn't exceed anybody else's expectations or invoke their judgment. This is probably not your best choice. Would you give up "longing to be" (belonging) in favor of being? Would you give up all the longing you have done? This means you will have to stop being a romantic and give up believing that everything will turn out fine.

You wait for somebody to come along who is attractive to you as though that's going to create the life you think you ought to have. But has anybody you have ever been attracted to turned out to be fun? You are a humanoid, so after the pheromones wear off, it becomes work. You attract the kind of person you are asking for and they show up exactly the way you think you want them to and then you say, "Wow, this person is boring too!" The problem is actually you. You are the boring one because you are not choosing a big enough life.

Part of the problem is you keep looking for attraction as a way of proving there's some part of you missing. Notice that we always look for somebody we are attracted to; seldom do we look at whether or not we are attractive. Why is that? What would it take to make you attractive?

In writing the list of the things you would like to have, you are actually writing a list of the things you would like to be and the things you believe you are not. You are looking for someone you are attracted to who will give you what you have decided you are not. Is it true that you are unattractive—or is that the lie you are perpetrating on yourself?

Get the energy of all the lies and logical lies you are perpetrating on you about how unattractive you truly be*? *Everything that is times a godzillion, will you destroy and uncreate it all, please? Thank you. Right and wrong, good and bad, POD and POC, all nine, shorts, boys and beyonds.*

Vibrational Compatibility

One of the things that creates a good relationship is vibrational compatibility. It's funny that when it actually shows up for you, most of the time you will say, "Oh, that was too easy." And if it's too easy, it can't be right. Vibrational compatibility feels like that ease. It is ease and space; it doesn't require anything.

How many "right" people have shown up in your life and you decided it was too easy, so you rejected them? If they are cute, you will put up with them a lot longer, but if they actually like you and adore you, you will not put up with them at all. Because the most boring thing in the world is someone who actually likes you and thinks you are cool.

* See Glossary for explanation of the use of the word *be*.

There was a lady who had a man who adored her and thought everything she did was perfect. Now she wasn't the perfect woman, she didn't have the perfect body, she didn't have everything going on in her life, but for this man, the sun rose when she arose and his life was perfect because she was in it. Could she have him? No. She had always thought she wanted a man who would adore her and now that she had one, could she receive it? No. Most of us have an illusion of what we would like someone to be for us, but we are not willing to see when somebody is willing to be this for us.

Have you ever given up men or women who actually like you in favor of people who don't? Isn't that cool? You get somebody who adores you and would lay down their life for you, and you say, "I'm sorry, you are too boring, go away." But men or women who disdain you and treat you badly are attractive to you.

Are you willing to look at the person in front of you? Or have you already decided they are what will work in your life? And then do you make them work like hell to get into your life?

Most people choose somebody who is not vibrationally compatible as though that is a real relationship, as though that is part of the attraction. You are attracted to somebody you believe has what you don't have as though that's a good idea, rather than asking, "What would it take to be with someone that expands upon what I already have and makes it greater?"

I asked the lady who had the man that totally adored her, "What's going to happen when this man is gone from your life and you realize he's the one you have always been looking for?"

She said, "What do you mean? Is he going to die?"

I said, "Maybe. But when he's gone from your life, will you long for him? When he's gone from your life, will you be willing to have him then?" She started to look at her relationship differently after that.

How do you find someone who is vibrationally compatible with you? Here is a question you can ask: What can I be, do, have, create, or generate that would make me vibrationally compatible with someone who would be expansive and joyful in my life? *Everything that doesn't allow that to show up, I destroy and uncreate it all? Right and wrong, good and bad, POD and POC, all nine, shorts, boys and beyonds.*

You can have vibrational compatibility with someone without actually having things in common with that person. Just ask the question: "Is this person vibrationally compatible with me? Yes or no?" And see which answer is lighter.

Vibrational compatibility is a different energy than attraction. It is an ease; it's a feeling of space in being when you are around someone. There is no need to force things that you would normally force with other people. You like their sense of humor, you think they are funny; you appreciate the smells of their body and you share a sense of what you like in life and what things are possible. If you're vibrationally compatible with somebody, there is a similarity in what you find valuable and joyful and fun even though you may have totally different tastes. When you are vibrationally compatible, what is valuable, joyful and fun is the operative state of being.

Vibrational compatibility is different from chemistry. Chemistry is where your body finds the person exciting, and it requires you to cut off your awareness to go there. When there is a lot of chemistry your brain goes away. You go "Wow!" and you turn off all your awareness so you can have sex with the person. You are going back into the 10% when you look for chemistry. It's not your brightest choice.

Would You Like to Live with This Person?

When we are attracted to someone, we do not ask, "Can I live with this person?" We say, "I am so attracted to this person. They are so wonderful and the sex is so good; I am so horny, I can't wait to touch their body, and I can't wait for them to touch my body, ooh, ah."

This has nothing to do with creating a great relationship. Relationship and sex have nothing to do with each other, but we act as though sexual attraction is the prelude to relationship. Before you consider getting into a relationship, it is important to look at the person you are with and see if you would actually like living with them.

Choosing the person you would like to have a relationship with is the same as going into the shop and seeing what you are not willing to receive. There is a difference between "Can I live with this?" and "Would I buy this?"

You will "buy" the person you would like to have a relationship with, but you never ask, "Can I live with this person?" Then somewhere down the road you find, "I can't live with this person, this is crazy!" Because you have already bought them, you have to make yourself right for having bought them and so you stay in the relationship no matter how bad it is. You can't return a relationship and get your money back!

What Would I Like to Choose for Me?

When you take on fixed points of view about relationship, you don't function from choice anymore. You put relationship into the box of what it's supposed to be rather than asking, "What do I really want to choose for me?"

If you did relationship and copulation from the question "Will this give me more of the joy and value of me?" that alone would change your life. Whether it's copulation or relationship or both, if you were to look for it to create the joy and the value of you, how different would that be from what you have been looking for so far?

People say they want a relationship that is x, y and z. Does the person they are choosing fit those criteria? No, but they believe that if they change them enough, they will fit. Sorry. That isn't going to work. Women think, "Once he stops doing this, once he starts doing this, once I get him to dress better, once he gets classier, it will be great." For men, it's usually, "Once I get her wanting to have sex more, everything will be okay." No. Look at what is.

Ask yourself, "Is who this person is—right now—increasing the joy and value of me?

Tool: Is This Rewarding?

If you are going to generate something new in your relationship, you can't have a judgment about something being good or bad because then you can only generate that which will match the judgment you already have.

Ask the question *"Is this rewarding?"* Rewarding is the generative universe. Ask, "If I do this, will this be rewarding?" If it feels light, go for it.

It's not a linear question. Don't try to make logical sense of it—because you will undo everything that is going to make it rewarding in the process of trying to figure out if it would be rewarding or why it would be rewarding. When you try to figure out *why,* you are trying to figure out the contextual reality of *why.* This requires you to judge it, which means you are no longer perceiving what is actually going on.

So you ask, *"Is this rewarding?"* If you get a *yes,* even if you don't see how it is rewarding, do it anyway. Eventually over time, you will begin to see, "Oh, this is what's occurring here. This is a piece of information I needed" or "This is a person I needed to meet." There may be times when you do something that feels rewarding and you lose money or things go wrong and then out of that, something else shows up that expands your world.

Don't keep trying to choose what's right. If it is rewarding to do something you can still ask, "Okay, do I truly wish to choose this?" Yes. "Do I want to choose this?" No. "Okay fine, I'm not going to choose it." Stay in the question.

Things are presented to you every day; an opportunity, somebody you have to talk to, somebody you have to do some work with. Do you have to do a whole lot of work? No. But you might choose to, if it seems to be rewarding. It is not about something being rewarding for them or rewarding for you, it is just rewarding. Even if you feel, "I'm exhausted. I don't have the energy for this. I don't want to do this," you may say, "It feels rewarding, so okay, I'll do it." It always turns out to be something that changes and expands some part of your life when you choose it.

Oftentimes, choosing something that is rewarding takes you from a place you have been comfortable into a place you are not comfortable, and in so doing you may meet someone who gifts something to you and contributes to your life in a way that is far greater than you thought possible.

If something is going to be rewarding but you also perceive some heaviness, what feels heavy is the awareness of the thing you are going to become aware of that you don't want to be aware of. The heaviness is, "I am going to have to receive something I have decided I don't want to receive!" The thing that will be rewarding is the opening of a door to receiving where you have been unwilling to receive in the past.

Chapter Seventeen

USING ENERGY TO ATTRACT

Why is it that when you are not trying to attract someone, you are attractive—and when you are trying to attract someone, you are not attractive? What is that about? It has to do with energy flows.

When you pull energy away from somebody, they think they are attracted to you. When you push energy at somebody, you are attracted to them.

Most of the world wants to be attractive. To be attractive requires you to pull energy from the person you want to attract. When you give energy to someone, they know you are attracted to them. Most men push energy at women to try to get them to lower their barriers and receive them or go out with them or have sex with them. It's the energy of "You want me, you want me, you want me."

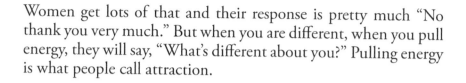

Women get lots of that and their response is pretty much "No thank you very much." But when you are different, when you pull energy, they will say, "What's different about you?" Pulling energy is what people call attraction.

Pulling Energy Attracts

Some people have a capacity to pull energy continuously. It is just part of how they operate, so everybody is attracted to them. Michael Jackson is a good example. Imagine Michael Jackson on stage performing. Is the energy going from the crowd to him or is the energy going from him to the crowd? In other words, is Michael Jackson pulling energy from the crowd or is he pushing energy at them? He's pulling energy like crazy and people can't take their eyes off him.

Michael wasn't cognitively aware of doing this; he just did it. He could never be filled up, which is why his life was so unhappy. He was always pulling energy and trying to get something he thought he was missing.

Michael Jackson, Madonna and a lot of "stars" need to pull energy all the time; they feel like they are missing something so dynamically that they suck everything from everyone as much as possible. And everyone says, "Oh, they are so attractive, they are so beautiful, they are so wonderful, I love them so much." Have you ever seen stars who did that all the time and then got married and suddenly they were not stars any more? What happened? Why are you not so attracted to them anymore? Because they felt fulfilled and they stopped pulling energy. Brad Pitt is a perfect example. He was always going, "Love me, love me, love me," then he finally got Angelina who said, "I love you," and he is no longer a big star. His stardom went away when he stopped pulling energy.

Pushing Energy Repels

Most men think that women are pushing energy at them when they are attracted to them, but that is not what is occurring. When someone pushes energy at you, it is intimidating and you feel like you need to withdraw from them. When you are attracted to a woman, it's because she is pulling energy from you. That's what makes you think you are attracted to her.

When you push energy at someone, they are often repulsed by you because it feels way too forceful. It is like a battering ram. You think you are not being attractive enough so you push harder and wonder why the person doesn't want anything to do with you.

The funny thing is that it's really easy to change that energetic flow. It is just a choice you make. You just say, "Well instead of pushing I'm going to pull." If you do that all the time, it creates a place where people notice you and feel drawn to you. You create a sense of mystery because people can't quite be sure where you are or what you are going to do next.

If you would like to play with this tool, here is one way of doing it. I have used this with great success. Years ago when I was young and beautiful, I used to invite women to my house for dinner. I would serve them a nice dinner, a great bottle of wine, I would have china and crystal and all the right stuff and then I would ask the lady questions about herself. Every time she would ask me a question about me, I would give a one-word answer and I would move on to asking more about her.

By the end of the evening she usually said, "Wow, you are the most interesting man I ever met" and I knew I was going to get laid. Why? She had decided I was interesting because I was interested in her. I would pull energy from her, I would ask questions about her and I never told her anything about me, ever. It is a mistake to tell people about you and what you are interested in. When she would ask, "What are you interested in?" I would answer, "I'm interested in everything; so what are you doing now?"

You may think that nobody would just sit there and talk about themselves all night, but 99% of people, once you ask them another question, will keep talking about themselves because they are the most interesting subject in their lives. They will be ecstatic that they have found somebody who's interested in them too.

Do you want to get laid? Be interested—never interesting. Realize that you are of no value and that they are of total value. When they are of total value and you talk to them, they will want to have your babies. It doesn't matter whether you want that or not! I'm sorry; it's not about you—ever! You have been living with the point of view that it's always all about you. Get over yourself! It is always all about them. They are the valuable product. Okay?

Maintaining Limitations Through Attraction

Are you satisfied with your life? No? Okay, so why do you keep choosing the same kinds of relationships? It is an energy you have chosen someplace; it is something you decided was attractive to you. The only way you can maintain the smallness of your life is by being attracted to that which maintains the limitations you already have. So what have you decided is all you can have?

Start by making a demand that even if you end up not having somebody in your life, even if you never get laid again, you are going to have a bigger life than you ever thought was possible. Here is a question you can use:

What kind of person would I attract if I was willing to have a life that was so much greater than what I'm currently living, that by having that, would necessitate being greater than I've been willing to be? *Everything that doesn't allow that to show up, I destroy and uncreate it all? Right and wrong, good and bad, POD and POC, all nine, shorts, boys and beyonds.*

The interesting thing is that when you make the demand, suddenly you are attracted to people who are different. Suddenly you are not attracted to people who want a limited life, who want a small life. You are attracted to people who are willing to have something greater.

Finding a Rich Man

A lot of women have told me they want a man who is rich.

I say, "Really? What kind of men do you choose?"

They say, "Poor men."

I reply, "Then that is a lie, isn't it? You are not really willing to have a man that is rich. You think you ought to have a man who is

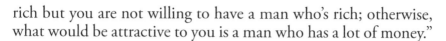

rich but you are not willing to have a man who's rich; otherwise, what would be attractive to you is a man who has a lot of money."

Most people live within the same structure as their family. If you came from a low upper class family or a middle class family or a low middle class family or a poor family, then you will choose people that match that vibration.

If you came from an upper crust family and you decided, "I never want to be like that" then you will always choose somebody who will never take you there. There is brilliance in that because you already know before you choose that person that they are not going to catapult you out of your small life. You already know that they won't ever do anything to take you out of your comfort zone and your standards. Is that weird? Because when you get into relationships where you create the place of limitation over again, you act like you didn't know it was going to happen. No, you knew it. That is why you are choosing it. Is that brilliant on your part?

Get the energy of all the people you have ever been attracted to as a way of maintaining the limitations you currently have. *Everything that is times a godzillion, will you destroy and uncreate it all, please? Thank you. Right and wrong, good and bad, POD and POC, all nine, shorts, boys and beyonds.*

What About Sexual Attraction?

Using energy to attract is not the same as sexual attraction. The truth is that as long as you are breathing you will be sexually attracted to someone. And if you are a man there will not be a woman you are not sexually attracted to! The lie is that you have

155

to do something about it when you find somebody sexually attractive.

First of all, you want to ask your body who it's attracted to, because your body is the one that has sex, not you. You, the being, stand outside and watch it happen. Your body is the one that gets to have all the sex. You are also aware of when the other person is thinking about sex and you often misidentify that what they are thinking is what you are thinking. Then you start trying to bend, fold, staple and mutilate yourself to fit in their world and that's what you call attraction.

Chapter Eighteen

WOMEN ARE FROM VENUS, MEN HAVE A PENIS

Dain and I made an interesting discovery at the first Sex and Relationship class we facilitated. The class was held over two nights and two days with the first night being for men only, the second night for women only and then the following two days were for both sexes together.

On the first night, the men were invited to get free of all their judgments of women. It was very successful and the men said things like, "I never realized I loved women so much."

The women came in the next night and were supposed to get rid of all their judgments of men. Unfortunately, the women went home after class that night and created a whole new batch of judgments about men that justified why they should kill them all. They came in the next day and cut the testicles off every man in the class. If you listen to the CDs of that class, you do not hear a man speak until almost four o'clock in the afternoon on the last day. They were all scared to death!

We began to realize something was going on that was different from what everyone thinks is true, and during that class we became aware that it is the women who want to conquer the world and be the warriors, not the men. Once they started acknowledging that fact, the women got brighter and happier.

Women say that men are trying to keep them down. Are you sure? How are you getting that? Is that really the way it has been in history? When there is a disaster it has always been "women and children first." Doesn't that make women the most valuable product on the planet? In a war, they kill all the men and keep the women. So who is important?

The reality is that men will cut off more of themselves to make a relationship work than women will. Most women just want to own a man. It's like having a pet. Does that idea amuse you? That's because you know it's true, don't you? Women will say, "No, I'm not doing that" and men will say, "What do you want me to do? I will do whatever you want, just let me see your golden vagina. Please let me worship it." Unfortunately that's the way it works.

Women Rule, Men Drool

When it comes to the initial contact between men and women, it is the woman who gets to choose who she wants. Men have been taught to wait for a woman to say, "Come here" before they can do anything. A woman chooses a man and the man says, "Oh my God! I'm chosen! What parts of me do I have to cut off in order to fit into your world?"

Please look around and see the truth of this. This is what is going on in the world. If you can get this, then you will stop trying to make yourself believe that it is different from what it is. If you look at the way things work, then you can have a different choice and a different reality. If you continue to believe in these other points of view, you are setting yourself up for a disaster.

We are not saying this is right or wrong or good or bad. Be willing to look at what's going on so that you can have whatever you would like to have. If you are willing to look at how people function in the world, then you will see how women create a situation that allows them to pick and choose. It is not right or wrong; it is just what occurs.

Men have been taught from the time they are little, "If you love me, you will do this for me." They know they are supposed to do something in order to prove their love. This is what boys learn from their mothers when they hear, "If you love mummy, you will do this for me."

Little girls hear from their fathers "Oh honey, it will be okay. I'll hold you tight and everything will be alright." So women are looking for somebody who will hold them and make them feel better and men are looking for somebody who will tell them what to do.

Most men expect women to tell them to do something and women expect men to deliver whatever they ask for. A man loves being able to do something for you because from his point of view, that is the way he shows you he loves you.

What most women want to do is to share their feelings with a man and talk to him. That's how they know they are loved. Women, there is something you need to understand: That is not what your man is for. A man is not wired to share everything with you. Have you girls ever tried to tell a man something just to share? "Oh my

God, you will never guess, but I had this terrible argument with Suzy today. It was just horrendous and I ended up screaming at her…" and the man says, "Okay, what can I do about it? Should I talk to her?" A man wants to know what he can do to fix it for you because that's how he cares. That's the way he shows you that he loves you.

Women are content to just talk about the argument. That's all that is required for them. If you are looking to share, ladies, you need to get a girlfriend.

It's true that there are some men who are girls. They want to talk about everything and they love to have their emotions. Some gay men are like that; however, there are also some men who are not gay who function like women. They have a hard time in relationships because they pick women who are like men and the relationship and the sex don't seem to work very well, because they are trying to be something they are not.

Men are looking for someone who will say, "Hey, come here. You are strong, I want you." Most men have been taught that they are not allowed to continue beyond the point where the woman says no, so they wait for the green light that says, "Come on, let's go!" The women sit there and say, "No, no, no, no…now." As long as you call him "lover," he knows his job is to get it up the moment you say yes.

In reality, women have all the control and they should know that. You girls should know that this is the way it works. Once again, we're not saying that this is a bad thing. You just have to know what you already have control over so that you can use it when you want to and so you have choice.

If you are not aware of this, you are going to make your choices from the point of view that you have no power when you actually have a lot of potency in this area. What tends to be perpetrated out there is that women are powerless and men are powerful. No. Ladies, you have the power, you have that potency and you do yourself a huge disservice if you believe the point of view society is perpetrating on you is actually true.

If you are a woman in business, show some cleavage and every man's head will go south for the winter and he'll do whatever you ask. Women say, "But I don't want to do that. I want to be known for my mind." It is great to be known for your mind, but in business it is a whole lot better to sell them what they want so you can own them. You want men to be so stupid that they'll give you whatever you want.

Look, it's the difference between functioning at the 10%, which is the "fair" point of view and functioning at the 990%. When you are in the 990%, are you at an unfair advantage? Absolutely! You are the only one on the playing field when you are functioning from the 990% and you can see exactly what you have to say to get someone to agree to whatever you ask. You wouldn't do that for what reason? Would it be too easy?

If you are willing to acknowledge this about yourself, you ladies will pick a man who will nurture and care for you, love you totally and be willing to support you in whatever adventure you decide to take on. As a humanoid woman, you want the adventure of life. Humdrum, normal, housekeeping? I don't think so. Do you humanoid women like keeping house? No thanks. Been there, done that!

Listen up, ladies! If you want a guy who's nice, get a gay friend. If you want somebody to share with, get a girlfriend. If you want a man who will do what you want, get a human. If you want a man who will take care of you, nurture you, and have sex whenever you ask, get a humanoid. But call him "lover," never "honey," "sweetie," or "darling," and always know what you are asking for.

The Other Sex

Become aware of talking about men and women as the *opposite* sex. Men and women are not the opposite sex; they are the *other* sex. When you say men or women are the opposite sex, you will find a way to be oppositional with them. You will create an opposition automatically, and that is not in your best interest if you really want to create a relationship. They are the other sex. As the other sex, they can contribute to your life.

The Value of Being Unavailable

There is a point of view out there that guys who don't care will score way more than guys who do. So if you are an uncaring asshole, you will have women all over you. Why? Because you are not available. The guy who is available—why would any girl want him? Obviously no one else does. Therein lies a woman's point of view. A woman will steal another woman's man because he has already been tried and tested. He must be good if somebody else wants him. He must be valuable, and not only that, if she gets him, she wins.

A woman will always go after a married man. Men will always go after a single woman. This is just the way it works; it's not a right or wrong. Why do women go after a married man or a man who's with another woman? Because women are the most competitive creatures on the planet.

Now once again, what if that weren't a bad thing? What if it was just part of what is that you haven't been willing to look at before? If you were actually willing to look at this, would it give you the freedom to be you and to choose what would actually work for you?

Most women in this reality have the point of view that if a man is willing to give himself to her utterly then he obviously has no value because he's not smart enough to realize that somebody else should want him. This is not one of our brightest moments, folks.

Girls, would you please get that, for a man, if you are breathing you are valuable. If you have a vagina and you have breasts, you are valuable. Men are cute; they are not bright. And once again, what if that weren't a bad thing?

Being a Mistress

There are cultures that encourage multiple partners in relationships. In Italian, Jewish, Argentinean, Portuguese and other Latin cultures, the ideal is that a man is supposed to have a wife and a mistress and cheat on the mistress. That makes him a real man, so there are a lot of men out there that have to have an affair on the side. Now if that works for you, what makes it wrong? All of those Mediterranean cultures are set up that way and you just have to know that this is the way they function. It is not important unless you are a woman who is going to marry one of these men and then you have to learn to make him pay for his infidelity with expensive jewelry.

For some women, being with a married man is perfect because you only have to see him when he can get away from his wife. He doesn't bug you and you don't even have to spend the night with him. If you want to do it, do it. Choice creates awareness. You do it once or twice and then you will know if you want to continue to be involved.

Remember, women always go after married men—and married men always go after single women. Men don't usually go after another man's wife. So if you are a single woman, a married man could go after you. It's weird, but that's the way it works.

The Object of Your Desire

Please learn to use words with an awareness of what the word means in the way you're using it. The word want means to lack. It does not mean to desire. Desire is something you think is going to be a future thing and not something you can have right now. If you were willing to have it now, could it arrive? Yes! Instead of saying, "I want this" or "I desire that," say "I'll have this" or "I'll take that" or "I'm going to create that in my life." Does that feel lighter and more like it could actually show up?

Desire is about something in the future that may never be attainable. Do you desire to be desirable? That means you will desire whoever doesn't desire you, because if you can get that, it means you are desirable. Unfortunately, it also means that as soon as the object of your desire finds you desirable, you won't desire them anymore.

What if your relationship was not based on want or desire? What if it was based on "What can I contribute? What choices do I have today? What are the possibilities?"

Chapter Nineteen

RELATIONSHIP AS CONTRIBUTION

Contribution is not a one-way street. It is not just when you give to others; it is also the contribution you will allow others to be to you. Contribution is not taking whatever somebody gives you but being willing to see that others will contribute to your life and make your life better if you are willing to receive.

Contribution is the willingness to be with someone and receive everything they are without requiring anything of them. A person who is being a contribution is someone who contributes to your life out of choice, not obligation.

When contribution is present in a relationship, you can work together and accomplish things in a short period of time. Each person knows what their strength is, they are willing to ask each other for anything and they don't need to be thanked or validated. For example, when Dain and I go horseback riding, we have to load the horses into the trailer. Dain is great at backing trailers up and I am great at handling horses, so he handles the trailer and I handle the horses. Everything gets done easily. I don't have to try to back up the trailer to prove I can do it. Can I do it? Yes. Can I do it as well as Dain? No. When somebody contributes to your life, they do what they are better at and you do what you are better at, and neither one of you has a point of view about it.

What often happens when you get into a relationship is you either try to prove you don't need the other person by doing things you are not that good at, or you ask them to do things for you and they begin to resent the fact that you are always asking them to do things you don't like to do. That is not being a contribution.

Giving 150%

Do you have the point of view that you have to give 150% in your relationship? Have you ever noticed that when you have that point of view, you manage to find somebody who takes 200%? No matter how much you give, they always take more and they don't give much back to you. Giving back to you is not part of their computation. If you have the point of view that you need to give 150% to have a relationship, you will always pull in somebody who will take from you. This is a good reason to approach relationship from the non-contextual point of view of contribution. Ask, "What can this person contribute to my life? What can I contribute to theirs?"

Do you realize you are spending about four minutes a day of quality time with yourself right now? Would you like to broaden that and enjoy the hell out of yourself for at least one hour a day? What a strange concept! What? I have to spend time with myself? But I am boring. Oops, that is a judgment. So how do you get to the point where you would like to spend more time with yourself and be happier with what you are getting? You ask a question: "What contribution can I be to my life today?"

By asking that question, you can receive the awareness of what the contribution might be. The more you ask that question, the more you can function from that point of view. After waking up and asking, "What contribution can I be to my life today?" enough times, you start to be that question and it starts to be part of your life. When you are willing to be a contribution to your life, you are willing to be present in it and to be a gift to you. If you are only spending four minutes a day of quality time with you, how much of a gift are you being to you?

The Energy of Contribution

You can be an energetic contribution to things that you have no tactile connection to. This includes your body, your business, your partner and all your relationships. If you are willing to acknowledge this, you will realize that you are asking for what's possible instead of assuming that possibility can only occur when you are there touching something, working on it or doing something to it physically.

The energy you are being is the contribution.

For example, let's say you have your own business. Before that business came into being, what was there? Just you, right? You were the energy that contributed the energy to the creation of the business. We tend to buy the lie that our contribution occurs only through our physical effort. That's not the case.

I run twenty-four businesses. I start out every day asking, "Okay, where do I need to put my energy today? Where do I need to put my attention? What needs to be handled that hasn't been handled?" I make telephone calls to all the places that are asking for attention and within an hour, I have handled everything that needs to be handled that day in those businesses.

People ask, "How do you do this?"

I say, "It is not a *how;* it is that I am always looking at what's possible, what choices I have, what question I need to ask and what contribution I can be."

When I'm in Australia, I can handle businesses that are in the USA, and when I'm in the USA, I can handle businesses that are in Australia. Even if I'm not making a phone call and directly connecting with that business, I am still energetically contributing energy to the businesses, which keeps everything continuously moving forward.

This also applies to your relationship. If you realize your contribution to the relationship is an energetic contribution that you be and that you don't have to be there physically, it opens up more options of how you can be with that person and also have your own life and be with yourself.

Chapter Twenty

FIGHTING FOR WHAT YOU WANT

Many people think they are choosing for themselves when they are actually choosing against someone else. They make choosing against someone else the basis of determining how to choose who they are. Are you making choices based upon objecting, rejecting, refusing, denying or fighting someone else's point of view? Does that make you a lover or a fighter? A fighter of course!

Who are you fighting? That would be you. You choose against yourself because you are not really choosing. You have determined you will fight everyone for everything so that you can have you. But fighting is not the way to have you, because if you fight everyone, that *everyone* includes you! Oops!

The other thing that fighting everyone creates in your relationships is that you will bring people into your life that you fight. You will only allow yourself to create relationships with people you can choose against, because you believe that is the only way of having you.

At one time, I worked with a six-year-old kid who was having trouble in school. This boy was fighting and getting into trouble with his teachers as a daily routine. His mother could not discipline him at all and asked me for help with her unruly son.

I asked the boy, "Do you like fighting?"

The little boy laughed and said, "Yeah."

I said, "Okay. So are you committed to fighting everyone?"

The kid said proudly, "Yeah."

I asked him, "Are you aware that *everyone* includes you?"

The boy looked at me for minute and then realized what I was saying. He said, "No!"

Then I asked, "So will you give up fighting everyone?"

The boy said, "Yeah!"

From that point on, the kid totally changed. He stopped getting into trouble at school and his mother found him much nicer to be around.

How much of your life do you feel like you are fighting yourself? Or having to fight the world in order to have whatever it is you would like to have? How much of your life feels like you against the world? *Would you like to give up fighting everyone now? Yes? Thank you. Right and wrong, good and bad, POD and POC, all nine, shorts, boys and beyonds.*

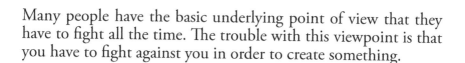

Many people have the basic underlying point of view that they have to fight all the time. The trouble with this viewpoint is that you have to fight against you in order to create something.

Is Being Competitive Working for You?

Were you taught you had to fight to get what you wanted in life? That is called competition. Did you resist being competitive (because you didn't like being competitive) even though you were told you were supposed to be competitive? Are you fighting against being competitive?

"I will not be competitive! I will compete!" How is that working for you? When you decide that you're not going to be competitive, you're already doing competition.

Instead you can start competing against yourself. I didn't like playing competitive sports, so I'd go ride horses, where I could compete against me. I was the only one who was as good at riding horses as I was. All I could do was compete at a level that was greater than what I did yesterday. When you do that, you start looking at how you can continuously improve, which is the only way that competition becomes something that expands your life and your reality. If you can make what you are doing better than what you have already done, you will expand your life and make it greater.

Don't divorce yourself to compete with somebody else. As a humanoid, you actually don't like competing against others. Humanoids may try to do competition with others, but it is never satisfying for them. Doing better than somebody else is like "So what?" There's nobody you can really compete with except yourself.

171

If you can do better than you did last time, then it is worth the win. Once you acknowledge the fact that the only person you really love to compete with is you, you may consider another possibility and go beyond competition.

As a humanoid, you want to be top of the list or you are not going to be happy. You are not content with being second level at anything, even if you have never tried it before.

The only exception to that is when you aim to come in second to make another person feel better by letting them win. When I was a kid, I would get into spelling bees and I would know how to spell the word but I also knew that if the other kid didn't win the point, he would be hysterical and devastated forever. So I would blow the word and let the other kid win the spelling bee. I could spell better than anybody in the class but I always got second in the spelling bee because I couldn't stand the fact that the other kid would be in tears if he lost.

Let's say that you have someone in your life who is nice and kind, but you are worried they might leave you. You don't want them to leave. How do you handle this? You pick the biggest loser you can find and you leave yourself. You divorce yourself so you don't have to leave them. If you pick the biggest loser, you're already a loser.

I had a friend who was upset because she hadn't had sex in a long time. She said, "I just want to get laid!"

I said, "So you want to get laid. This guy, this guy and this guy would gladly have sex with you."

She said, "Ugh! They're losers!"

"Really," I asked, "Who's a winner? The guys that won't have sex with you?"

"Yes."

I said, "Oh, so in other words, there are winners and losers. What about the people in between?"

"They don't count," she replied.

I said, "So we have winners, losers and no-counts. What choices do you have when there are winners, losers and no-counts? All you can do is go after the guys who won't have you so you can prove that you're a loser. How is that choosing for you?"

She got rid of her judgment of winners and losers and no-counts, and now she has a relationship for the first time in her life with a nice man—not a man who hates her and vilifies her body. She was not by any means a Skinny Minnie, but she would always choose guys who were super buff and super good looking and super everything. These guys wanted the Skinny Minnies and the models to prove they were potent and desirable because they could get the beautiful girl. My friend would do everything she could to be kind, caring and loving to them and the models would be mean and nasty, but the guys still went for the models. They thought that the person who rejected them was the winner—not the person who received them, loved them and cared for them. It's an insane reality we live in.

Yes, you will choose the biggest turd in the cesspool to have a relationship with. That's because you want to have it all, you want to take the big things in life, true or false? So you will pick the biggest turd or the biggest peach. But it doesn't matter to you as long as it is the biggest! The truth is that you can choose anything. You can choose it all.

The reality is that competition doesn't really exist. You as a competitor will always try to best yourself. Even in things like swimming competitions, the guy who wins is the guy who bests his own last record, because everybody else is competing against that guy's record. He's not competing against the other people; he's competing against what he did last time so he can do better. Humanoids are like this; they only like to compete against themselves.

You Don't Have to Fight

What would you like to create as your life? If you want a relationship, then learn how to get the relationship you desire. I was facilitating a class and there were three women in that class, all of whom had been marginally successful in their lives, and they were talking about wanting a relationship. I said, "You girls have to go out and marry a rich man. This is where you go and this is how you do it."

Within six months, all of them were making more money in their jobs, they were totally happy to be by themselves and they were having a great time. Why? Because I had given them permission to marry a rich man. They had been fighting the fact that their mothers had told them to marry a rich man, and once they no longer had to fight it, they could choose for themselves. If you girls are not looking to marry a rich man, you are going to find a poor one and then you are going to be pissed at him for not having money.

We tend to fixate on what we think we are supposed to have—or not supposed to have, thinking that if we fixate on it, we'll eventually make something work. When I suggested to these women that they get a rich husband, I said, "You have created a stunning body, you have got a beautiful face and you are intelligent. You are everything a trophy wife is supposed to be. Now, why don't you go out there and manipulate a man to do what you want?" Did they marry rich men? No, they went out and created their lives. They could do this because they stopped seeing "marrying money" as a wrongness; instead of making their mothers wrong for wanting them to marry a rich man, they said, "I can do that? I guess I could! Okay, is that what I desire? What would I like to choose today?" None of them married a rich man because that isn't what they truly wanted. What they wanted to do was to create their lives. They wanted a relationship with themselves where they weren't divorcing themselves in favor of something else.

The target here is to function from choice and not go against what might be possible for you in order to prove that you are right or that someone else is wrong. Proving is not choice. So how do you get to the point where you have choice?

You have spent your whole life "fighting against," so it may take a while to undo that, but you can help it along by asking a question like this when you seem to be in no choice: "Who or what am I fighting today?"

If you are fighting, you are not in awareness. Fighting for anything is always a lack of awareness, because in order to fight for or against something, you have to cut off every awareness that doesn't match what you're fighting for or against.

This happens everywhere. Throughout my life, I have looked at the choices people made and asked, "Why would people choose that? That's frigging nuts!" The things they chose made no sense to me. But I had a romantic illusion that love conquered all and everything would work out in the end. I had delusional points of view that everything would change for the better. It didn't.

I watched again and again as people chose things, and instead of making their life fabulous and amazing, their choices turned their life to crap. And then they would try to make the fact that their life was crap right. They would never say, "You know what? My life is crap. I'm not doing this anymore." Instead they would say, "Oh well, I chose, therefore I'm stuck with the choice I made." How about asking a question like: "What choice do I really want?"

Chapter Twenty-One

ASKING FOR WHAT YOU DESIRE

Women will do sex to get relationship and men will do relationship to get sex. When you keep thinking you want something in a relationship and it's not what you'd actually like to have, you keep creating it so it won't work because it's not what you would really like to have. If the things you really wanted in your relationship were not a wrongness in your eyes and you were okay with it, then you will be willing to ask for it and you would create a situation that actually works for you and the other person.

For example, there are many men (and some women) who would be happy to come over and have sex with you periodically and then go away. If you would like to do that, just say so. State what you want. "I really appreciate the fact that you are interested in me but what I am interested in is this kind of relationship. If that will work for you then we can go out again, if not, well that's fine and bye-bye."

State what you want and then let the other person have this thing called choice. We tend to hold back from asking for what we would actually like rather than saying it and then giving the other person choice. It is actually kinder to be clear and it will open doors to greater possibility for both of you if you are brave enough to try it.

Dain experienced this firsthand. He says, "At one point I was going out with a girl and from my point of view we were just having fun sex when I was in town, and that was great. That was not her point of view. It was not easy for me to summon up the courage to say what would actually work for me, but I knew I had to because she had begun to make it clear she wanted a relationship.

So I said to her, 'I totally get that you want a relationship, and that doesn't work for me at this point. I thought this was about the fun sex we talked about in the beginning. So I'm going to go now. We can keep having the fun sex if you want to.'

She said, 'No, I don't want to do that if you're not going to do relationship with me.'

I said, 'Okay, thank you so much,' and I left.

She was upset and pissed off at me for about three months. I totally got that because she thought it was going to be a relationship and I didn't say anything to clarify that. About three months later, she called and said, 'I just want you to know that by you choosing for you and saying what you said, you opened up doors for me to know that I can choose for me too. I also know that it's okay if I want a relationship. Thank you so much because I've been playing a twisted game with you and every guy I've ever gone out with and now I'm going to actually ask for what I want.' She's been choosing more for her in her life ever since."

Not Getting What You Asked For

Have you been choosing what you think you want and not succeeding in getting it? And then you think something is wrong with you? How is that working for you? If you recognize that what you are looking for is one thing and what you are getting is another, you can ask, "How come I don't get what I think I want? What am I not being or doing that would allow me to get what I say I want?" There is something you are not being or something you are not doing that keeps you from getting what you say you would like to have.

Now is the time to ask the question: "Okay is this what I truly desire? Is this truly what I would like to have in my life—or am I lying to myself?" This is the time to be bluntly honest. Notice when you cut off your awareness so you can get away with something. That strategy never works. If you want to change anything, first of all you have to claim, own and acknowledge what is really going on.

How many times do you choose the exact same relationship as though it is different each time? This is one of the places where you have to get bluntly honest with yourself: "Oh good, I keep choosing the same wrong person over and over again! What is that about?" You keep choosing the wrong person because it guarantees you don't have to be in a relationship. "Am I choosing the wrong person so I won't have to see that I love the wrong people—or am I choosing the wrong person because I really don't want to know what I'm doing?"

Tool: What Will He (or She) Be Like in Bed?

Here is a tool that can create huge change in your awareness around what you are choosing in relationships. Look at the person you are interested in and tap into their world. Ask this as an energetic question: **"What would he (or she) be like in bed?"** and you will gain awareness of everything that person is willing to be in relationship.

When you are willing to see what someone is going to be like in bed, you will know what the relationship you are going to have with them will be like. I had a lady do this with her children. I asked, "So what would it be like to go to bed with your daughter?"

She said, "I could never do that!"

I said, "No, no, just tell me what it would be like to go to bed with her."

She said, "Well, she would be totally self-centered. I would be of no value to her and she would actually have nothing to do with me. It would all be about her."

I then asked, "So, what is she like in your relationship?"

The mother said, "That's the perfect description of our relationship!"

I asked, "And what would your son be like in bed?"

She said, "Oh, he'd be all about nurturing me, taking care of me and making me feel special."

I asked, "Is that any different than your relationship with him?"

"No," she replied.

From that conversation, she gained awareness of what it would take to change her relationship with her daughter. Before that she hadn't been able to see it.

Sex is how you do receiving in this reality. When you see that this person is going to be self-centered, self-absorbed and not interested in you, that is about their receiving. This lady always had to give to her daughter all the time. She had no point of view about herself. She could not be in the computation of anything that involved her daughter.

When she realized the self-centeredness was not serving her daughter in becoming a better person, she stopped allowing that to be the way she related to her daughter. She started to say, "No, I need to receive from you. You need to give to me. I'm going to ask you for this now." And in so doing, she got her daughter to be a person who could give and take instead of only take. Had she continued to allow her daughter to be just a taker, the girl would have ended up being a very unhappy and manipulative person. Now she's a sweetheart. She has turned into a great kid.

If you are a man, you have to be willing to ask this question about men as well as women. You are not usually vested in getting laid when you look at another man, so there are no barriers or points of view in the way of you receiving awareness from them. But because you are vested in getting laid with women, when you see a woman you think is attractive you won't receive the energy from her for fear she might turn you down. You cut off your willingness to receive the awareness by being vested in the outcome.

If you are a woman, the best way to find out what a man would be like in bed is to practice looking at other women and asking, **"What would that woman be like in bed?"** Because you are not actually interested in going to bed with the woman, you can ask and get the awareness of it. This will let you practice how to ask for and get the awareness of this around men.

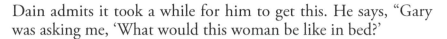

Dain admits it took a while for him to get this. He says, "Gary was asking me, 'What would this woman be like in bed?'

I'd say, 'I don't know!' I just couldn't get it.

So Gary said, 'Okay, let's try something else. What would this man be like in bed?'

It took a little clearing for me to actually even look at this, but after Gary worked with me for a while, I was able to describe what that would be like.

Then Gary asked, 'Okay what about this guy? What about this guy? What about this guy?' and then after about twenty of them he asked, 'What would this woman be like in bed?' And I was able to see it easily. Okay cool! Once I got over my investment in the outcome and the points of view I had, I could see the energy of it.

I realized the difficulty was that I knew if I looked and saw what it was going to be like and it was something I didn't want, then I wouldn't choose that person as somebody I'd go to bed with. And I didn't want to *not* be choosing people to go to bed with. I wanted to leave as many options open as possible, even if it would suck."

You're the One I Want

What question is, "I want you?" It is not a question; it is a decision and a conclusion. You might want to ask, "Will this person desire to have me in their life? And if so, in what capacity? Do they want to use me occasionally or do they want to abuse me?" There are some women who like to abuse men. There are some men who like to abuse women. That's what they consider sexual foreplay. It's just what some people like. You've got to be willing to ask questions or you won't know these things and you'll pick people who will do that kind of stuff. You will cut off your awareness just because you feel "Ooh, this one is kind of vibrationally compatible. This could be good!"

Ask on an energetic level about what will work for you in the relationship and be bluntly honest with yourself about what you want. Then you have to ask, "What do they want? And can I provide what they desire?" Ask energetically (not directly) because everyone will lie if you ask directly.

What would you really like to have as your life in a relationship? How much contribution do you want from someone else?

Women who say, "I want a man who will adore me forever" are talking about their father. Men will pick women that are just like their mothers. Those relationships are destined to fail. I have worked with many women who see their father as their relationship ideal, and I always ask, "How much is this man like your father?"

They will say, "Totally!"

I will say, "Okay then. How much sex are you having?"

"None!"

"Would you have sex with your father?"

"Well, of course not."

"Good, that's why you're not having sex with this guy."

"Oh my God, that makes total sense!"

This is the reason you have to get bluntly honest about what you want; otherwise, you will do this kind of thing. Get clear about "What am I really asking for here? Do I want somebody who will adore me or do I want someone who will contribute to generating a more extraordinary and phenomenal life than I've ever had?" That's a totally different thing than somebody who will adore you.

What are the possibilities here? What choices do I have? What questions can I ask? What contribution can I be and receive here? You can apply these questions to everything; the work you would like to have, where you would like to live, the life you would like to have, what you would like to be doing in life, what would be fun for you—everything.

When choosing a relationship of any kind ask, "Will this person contribute to my life?" If you get no, and they won't contribute to your life, why would you spend any time with them?

Saying No

One time many years ago, Dain went on a business trip and there was a pretty girl at the front desk of the hotel where he was staying. She kept flirting with him so he invited her out for dinner. During dinner she said, "I just broke up with my boyfriend and I know someday I'm going to have a relationship that will be even better than the last one." Dain's response was, "Well, all I'm interested in is sex for the fun of it."

After dinner Dain asked her, "Would you like to come to my room?"

She said, "Sure, I'd love to."

So they begin to get naked and playful and then she said, "I just want you to hold me." So he did. All night. His body felt like it was being sucked so hard it would turn into a prune—and he got more and more pissed off. He was pissed because he had agreed to divorce himself to give her what she wanted, which he thought was going to lead to sex. What she wanted was not what he wanted. He gave up what he wanted in favor of trying to make her happy, thinking that maybe somewhere during the night she would change her mind.

Around six in the morning, he woke her up and said, "I have to go do stuff today. Thank you so much, bye, bye," then he called me and said, "What do I do?"

I said, "So why didn't you say 'I'm sorry, that doesn't work for me. You can go home now'?"

Dain was amazed. He said, "You can do that? I had no clue you could tell a woman *no* to anything she asked for, ever!"

I said, "I'm going to be the girl and I'm going to ask, 'Could you just hold me all night long, please? I just want to be held. I want a relationship not casual sex.'" I pretended to be a girl and Dain was still having trouble saying, "No, that doesn't work for me." It took him twenty minutes before he could stammer it out. It took me an hour of asking him again and again before he could firmly say, "I'm sorry, that doesn't work for me. Could you go home now?"

That experience created choice for Dain. Prior to that his point of view was, "Well, if I'm with a woman we have to have sex." After that he could choose to hold her all night if he wanted to do that. If it was going to be nurturing for him and nurturing for her, he could do that. From Dain's point of view, he was impelled to have sex, sex, sex. When he became willing to say, "I'm sorry, that doesn't work for me. Could you go home now," he realized he could also say, "Hey, that works for me just fine. Come on in. I'd be happy to hold you."

There are a lot of men who do enjoy holding women. They enjoy the caring, nurturing space of being a man. It is one of the lies we buy into that for men it's just about sex. That is an impelled point of view that men feel they must function from.

Chapter Twenty-Two

IT'S ALL IN THE FAMILY

Before the Age of Two

When you come into this world and up until about two years old, you don't realize there is any difference between you and your parents. You think you are them, so you think like them. You are on the same wavelength and because you have to find out how to function in the world, you try to align your brainwaves with theirs. You figure you have to function the way they function. The fact that they are dysfunctional never enters your mind. This means you create brainwaves that put you on automatic pilot.

You take in everything they are and everything their relationship is in totality. If your dad was mad at your mom for getting pregnant or your mom was mad at your dad for getting her pregnant, you will always know that this is the way you are supposed to create a relationship.

I have worked with many men who had a hard time being with women and I found that it often got down to what happened with mom and dad when they were two years old. One man said his mom told his dad that she never wanted him to touch her again. So how many women had this man chosen who didn't want him to touch them? All of them! Whatever it is your mother and your father had as a relationship before you were two is your conditioned response for your current and future relationships.

If you had two sets of parents you are doubly in trouble because you are looking at both sets and you could spend your entire life trying to reconcile the disparate points of view. As a kid you come in with the point of view that your parents have been around longer than you so they must know better and they must be right. You come in trusting your parents rather than looking at them and asking, "Are they as bright as I am—or are they really dumb?" You don't ask that question. You will immediately go into the rightness or the wrongness of you.

Have you tried to raise your children from your parents' point of view? Are you still trying to raise yourself from your parent's points of view? Are you trying to prove your parents wrong? At around age two you learned the wonderful word *no,* but before that you thought you were your parents and your parents were you, which means that everything you currently dislike about them, you have already become. When you fight your parents, it means you get to fight you. It doesn't work very well, does it? You end up in conflictual universes, conflictual realities and conflictual paradigms as though they equal who you are.

How much of who, what, where, when, why and how you are is actually your parents point of view that you never even realized was your point of view before the age of two? *Everything that is, times a godzillion will you destroy and uncreate it all, please? Thank you. Right and wrong, good and bad, POD and POC, all nine, shorts, boys and beyonds.*

Kids Are Psychic

Most people feel that marriage and children are a trap. As a child, you are highly psychic and highly aware, and if you have a parent who says, "I wish I hadn't had children; I would have had the freedom to do what I wanted; I wouldn't have to be in this marriage; I wouldn't have to stay in this job," you pick up that energy even if you don't hear the words. The people around you have weird points of view, and because you are psychic, you pick it all up and believe *their* points of view are *your* points of view—and that's what you create your life from. You pick it up and at the same time, you try not to acknowledge the point of view about marriage and kids being a trap, which keeps you in the same conundrum of feeling that if you get married and have children, you are going to be trapped.

You have to admit what you know. You knew when you were two years old that you could read information out of your mother's head. You are an infinite being who knows all kinds of things, but you have to cut off huge amounts of awareness in order not to know that you know that you know. It is imperative that you acknowledge this or you will never get free and have choice on your own.

I worked with a lady whose oldest brother died when she was two. She became the head of the family because her mother was extremely distraught as a result of the death of her child. To this day, the lady doesn't have a relationship or a family; she got stuck being the mother of the family at age two. What about living her life?

Has your family made a single great trauma the reason and justification for the life you could not live and choose? How many projections, expectations, rejections, separations and judgments were put on you by your family to keep you from being you? Godzillions! *Everything that is, times a godzillion, will you destroy and uncreate it all? Yes? Thank you. Right and wrong, good and bad, POD and POC, all nine, shorts, boys and beyonds.*

This is not about trying to blame your parents for the way your life is. This is about recognizing you were psychic and aware when you came in and you knew more then than you do now. The target here is to get you to stop blaming you. If you as a kid come in wanting to make your parents happy and they won't get happy, who are you going to blame? Them or you? That would be you!

Making Your Parents Happy

If you are not able to make your parents happy, then you will choose a mate who is just like your parents and try to make him or her happy in the hopes that you will not be the failure you've already defined yourself to be at the age of two.

You could have picked a really nice person who was the best parts of your parents too. So it's not about blaming your parents for what doesn't work, because when your parents have a relationship that is working, you will pick someone who is the best parts of them rather than somebody who is the worst. It is only when you feel like you don't get enough love from one of your parents that you will always pick somebody who is like them so you can heal the relationship.

All the things you've done to make your relationships about what you learned before the age of two and all the projections and expectations, separations and rejections and judgments that were put on you about relationships before the age of two, *will you destroy and uncreate all those? Yes? Thank you. Right and wrong, good and bad, POD and POC, all nine, shorts, boys and beyonds.*

Which Parent Loved You Least?

Many people have one parent who didn't express his or her love in any way, shape or form so they go through life picking one partner after another who is like that parent. They're trying to find a solution to the fact that they couldn't make the parent love them. They think that if they ever finally get that love, it will solve their problem with that parent. They assume they're the problem. The fact that the parent didn't give love or receive love might be the real issue, but they don't have the opportunity to see that.

Look at your life and ask, "Which of my parents didn't love me the way I wanted them to love me?" It could also be a stepparent, an aunt or uncle, a grandfather, anyone. Then ask, "How many people do I pick to have a relationship with that are just like that person?" Is it more than one? Probably many more than one! Why? You have figured you have to heal that relationship before you can have what you desire.

Many people create relationships based on a point of view they have about the parent they feel didn't love them, believing that if they can actually get this person to love them, then they will have the value they have been seeking their entire life and they will be okay. It's not true. It's actually totally insane, because your attraction is always going to be to someone as that parent. It can also be that you will choose a woman who is like your father or a man who is like your mother.

In my case, I kept choosing women who were the same, yet they were not like either of my parents. I kept trying to figure this out. I asked, "Who is the one parent who didn't love me?" and I finally realized it was my stepfather. I saw that both of my ex-wives were just like my stepfather. Everything got clear. I was trying to heal a relationship with my stepfather, which was a relationship I did not desire in the first place. My stepfather was the only person in my family I could never get along with. He always disliked me. What did I do? I married two women who disliked me.

How much of you did you divorce when that parent figure didn't love you the way you wanted to be loved? A lot or a little? A lot! *Everything you did to divorce you from you so your parents would love you, will you destroy and uncreate all that? Yes? Thank you. Right and wrong, good and bad, POD and POC, all nine, shorts, boys and beyonds.*

The Sexualness of Caring

Why does a parent not love you the way that you want them to? One of the components of true caring is sexual energy, and for a parent to feel sexual energy towards a child is inappropriate. So parents turn themselves off and try to make you wrong. They try to turn you off too, so the sexual energy won't be there. But in order to cut off the sexual energy towards you, they also have to eliminate a huge part of the caring they could have for you.

Sexualness is the energy of living. It is what you feel in nature. It's the healing, caring, nurturing, creative, expansive, orgasmic energy that is the natural quality of life. It is totally joyful.

You start out as a sexual being, and that continues until you are about eight years old. It then begins to change as the downpour of people's judgments begins to erase the sexualness that's part of your being. If you buy into the idea that sexualness is a bad thing, you will withdraw it and define yourself by a limited sexuality rather than being the expansiveness of sexualness you can truly be.

For your body to be alive and vibrant, you have to allow sexual energy into your body. When you turn off your sexualness, you take the caring, nurturing, and healing away from your body and your life; you degenerate your body into death and you turn your sexual awareness into sexuality, which is about judgment. You end up replacing your sexual awareness with judgment of you, by you.

Children are full of sexual energy. They love their bodies and have no point of view about enjoying everything they can do with them. They play and laugh and everyone is drawn to that energy of sexualness. A father will feel that energy and go, "I can't believe I'm having sexual thoughts about my son." Then he makes himself and his son wrong for it and he has to create distance in the relationship ever after.

How much of you did you divorce in order not to be a sexual being that would turn everybody on? A lot or a little? A whole lot! *Everything you did to divorce you from you, will you destroy and uncreate all that? Yes? Thank you. Right and wrong, good and bad, POD and POC, all nine, shorts, boys and beyonds.*

If you are a parent, recognize that your kids are highly sexual when they come in. When you hold a little baby, isn't their skin so soft you want to touch it with total sensualness? Of course! That is part of the sexual energy a baby is willing to be. As a parent you look at your kids and you say, "Whoa, you are so amazing!" which is really saying, "What a sexy little devil you are!" The energy feels the same doesn't it? You believe that something about this energy is wrong and feel you have to turn it off. The truth is that as a parent, you have a choice between pretending that you don't see it and that it isn't exciting to you or acknowledging your child's sexual energy without judgment. What if you were willing to never withdraw that energy? Would that give your children a different view of their sexualness?

This whole area of sexualness is so filled with misinformation that unless you have some of these tools, you won't know what to do with it. If you have been creating your relationships based on the parent who loved you the least, what can you do to change it? Well, first of all, acknowledge that this is what you have been doing. Then look at the person you are now interested in and ask, "Is this person another one of these parent figures?" Then ask, "Truth, did I desire to have sex with that parent? Did they desire to have sex with me?" Yes or No? What feels lighter? You don't have to do anything with this awareness except acknowledge it. There is no need to judge it as right or wrong. It is just what is. Acknowledging it as just what was there at the time allows you to change the position you have taken about it and get some freedom with it.

Everything that brings up, will you destroy and uncreate all that? Yes? Thank you. Right and wrong, good and bad, POD and POC, all nine, shorts, boys and beyonds.

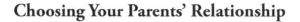

Choosing Your Parents' Relationship

Without even noticing, you may pick a partner that's like one of your parents. Maybe you hate your father but at the same time you know you are supposed to love him. So you love him while hating him and you pick somebody who's like him so you can love him while hating him too.

Any judgment you have eliminates your ability to perceive anything that doesn't match your judgment. That's the problem with judgment. As soon as we take a judgment, anything that doesn't match it cannot come into our awareness. Anything that doesn't match that point of view is something we can't be and can't deliver. It's something that can't be in the relationship.

If you judge and define someone as "just like my parent," then anything that doesn't match that point of view is something you can't see. It seems unbelievable, but that is the way it works. The power and potency we have to eliminate what would be nurturing, valuable and amazing to us is beyond our wildest expectations. We prevent ourselves from receiving by the judgments we have.

If you recognize that you are choosing the person you are in relationship with because you had a problem with a parent and you are trying to solve that, you can ask, "Who am I really with, that isn't my parent?" Ask the question and you will start to see the person as they really are.

Becoming Your Parents

When you look at your parents, do you think, "I should have a relationship because relationship is good?" Or do you think "Well, no wonder I didn't want a relationship! And I was thinking there was something wrong with me!" Your emotional point of view about what it means to have a relationship is based on what you saw your parents do and whether they were emotionally satisfied with one another.

If you are looking for emotional satisfaction you will have to re-create the trauma and drama your parents went through because that is the only criterion you have for what is emotionally satisfying. So the only person you can have in your life that would work for you is somebody who is exactly like your parents; which means you would have to become like them too.

You have a hard time not becoming your parents when you have children because that's the only example you have of what a parent is. I swore to myself that I would never be like my mother in raising children and I would never treat my children the way my mother treated me. Then one night at two a.m., I was awakened by my eldest son and his friends, who were laughing loudly in the living room. I marched into the living room and said, "Okay young man, do you realize you have to be at work at six o'clock in the morning and you're not being responsible and…" I stopped mid-sentence as I had the sudden awareness that I had become my mother, then I continued, "and my mother said this same thing to me and I ignored her too. Good night!"

Family is an acronym for **F**ucked up **A**nd **M**ainly Interested in **L**imiting **Y**ou.

You Choose Your Parents

Who created your body? You or your parents? The reality is you slammed your parents together at the right moment to make your body. I know this is true from my own experience. I woke up in the middle of the act of having sex and ejaculated almost instantly after awakening. I have never had that experience except for the two times pregnancy occurred. Literally, we were in the act before I was awake. Both of us were asleep and the next thing you know, we had a baby!

This is what beings do. They say, "Okay, if they get together right now I'll create the body I want." So they create the body they want and then say to their parents, "I can't believe you made this stupid body for me." You sat out and watched until exactly the right moment to get the body you wanted, so if you are not happy with it, get over yourself!

You, as a being, know what the first ten years of your life is going to be before you come in to your body. You know what's going to occur and you are prepared for that. You choose parents you can control in one way or another, parents who will never ask you to be anything more than you have decided you wish to be. Then you start to get bored and you demand of them "Why don't you ask me to be something greater?" They can't. You chose them for the fact that they would never ask you to be more than you were. Then you act like you can't be greater than you are because you don't have their permission, approval or support.

So if You Were You, Who Would You Be?

How much of your life do you try to make yourself into your parent's child instead of creating you? A lot, a little or mega-tons? *Everything that is, will you destroy and uncreate it all? Yes? Thank you. Right and wrong, good and bad, POD and POC, all nine, shorts, boys and beyonds.*

If you were not your parent's child, who, what, when, where and why would you be? Do you realize how much you limit your choices of how and where you live and what you do based on your parents point of view? You will choose either for them or against them. *Everything that is, will you destroy and uncreate it all? Yes? Thank you. Right and wrong, good and bad, POD and POC, all nine, shorts, boys and beyonds.*

Would you get that you are not your parent's child and that you chose them because their genetic material worked for you? That's the only reason you liked them and it's fine to divorce them—unless you actually like them or you could potentially inherit some money, in which case you might want to keep them.

Chapter Twenty-Three

OUT OF CONTROL WITH CHILDREN

Your kids choose you. They choose you because you will not demand of them the one thing they don't want to deliver. Eventually, however, they will demand it of themselves. This is the way humanoids do it, and sometimes you will wait until you are old before you demand it of yourself.

My parents demanded that I be normal, average and real. The one thing my parents would never ask of me was to stand out from the crowd. I chose them for that reason, but eventually I got to the point where I couldn't stand being part of the crowd.

Your kids came in knowing they can control you. Have they done a good job? Yes. They control you very well. And you keep thinking you have some credence in their life. They came in knowing they could control you; they control you utterly and you pretend that they don't. How delusional do you have to make yourself to believe that they don't control you?

Giving Kids Money

Do you have kids that always want you to prove that you love them? How do you prove that you love them from their point of view? Give them money. If you don't give them money then you don't love them, but if you do give them money, you are stupid. So you have to play this wonderful game with your children where you give them money at certain times and you withhold it at other times. The trick is not to withhold it on the issues that are important to them; only withhold it on the unimportant issues.

I Don't Want to Go to School

Unfortunately school systems often employ huge amounts of intimidation or force designed to get people to walk, talk and do all the things that are supposed to be done according to the standards they have. Humanoids in particular always rebel in that system.

What do you say when your kids don't want to go to school? I told my kids, "You don't have to go to school. The difficulty with that is if you don't go to school, other people are going to think you're not capable of anything. You will have a hard time convincing somebody you're talented enough to actually do anything un-

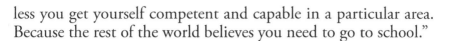

less you get yourself competent and capable in a particular area. Because the rest of the world believes you need to go to school."

If you ask your kids questions about what they wish their life to be like, they can make different choices about school. Ask, "What would you like to have as your life?" and get them to look at what they would really like to generate in life rather than what they want to be.

When I was a kid, I was asked, "What do you want to *be* when you grow up?" I usually replied, "Happy." *Being* is different from *doing,* but the world functions from the point of view that you have to do in order to be. When I would say that I wanted to be happy, they would say, "No, no, no, son, what do you want to *be* when you grow up? Do you want to be a doctor, a lawyer or an Indian chief?"

I would reply, "Yeah, as long as I'm happy."

You can ask your kids, "How much money would you like to have in your life? Are you more likely to get it by going to school or not?" These kinds of questions empower your kids to choose for themselves.

You also have to have allowance for you. Make your kids aware of your choice in this. "If you want to quit school, I will stop supporting you. This means you will have to get a job. The only place that would hire you at your age is probably McDonalds, so maybe you ought to consider waiting just a little longer and seeing what else you can learn that will make people think you're smarter than they are, and then they'll pay you a lot of money for being smarter."

One could argue that there are some multi-millionaires that never finished school, and this is true, but they are not multi-millionaires because they didn't go to school. They are multi-millionaires because they are humanoids who were willing to jump to 12% to 15% and who did not live in contextual reality. If your kids wish to be successful, that's what they have to be willing to do as well—jump to the 12% to 15%.

To the multi-millionaires who never finished school, non-contextual reality is real. They said, "This sucks, I see that this sucks, I'm not going to live like this." In other words, they made a demand—and then they asked, "What else is possible? What choices do I have? Who do I have to question? What do I have to learn? What can I contribute? What would contribute to where I want to go?" That's non-contextual reality.

Am I Raising My Children Right?

Sometimes in a family, you will see one kid who wants to go out and help the world. This is a kid who has a desire for something greater in life, and there will be another kid—same parents—who wants to live on the streets. This is not an indication that how you rear a child equals the result; each person comes in as the person they are from the very beginning.

If a person wants to be miserable and awful, you can't change it. If they want to be wonderful, fabulous and amazing, you can't change that. There are people who have been abused so horribly that they should have become the vilest people in the world, but they are not. They have been sexually abused, physically abused, mentally abused and financially abused. Every form of abuse has been done to them, and they still come out as kind, loving, caring people.

There are also kids from the same family who got the same kind of abuse and they perpetrate that abuse on the next generation. What's the difference? The being. The being is the determinant, not the way they were raised. You can take a fixed point of view about this—or you can look at what is actually occurring here and see what creates this determination. It always boils down to the infinite being and what they are choosing. If they want to choose to live on the streets, they choose to live on the streets.

Parents who have used Access Consciousness tools for a number of years find that as their kids grow up, they choose *not* to take drugs, *not* to do heavy alcohol and not to try to turn off their awareness. That's because their parents acknowledge the psychic awareness their kids have. When parents do this, the kids don't think they are wrong for having all the information they have and they can chose differently.

The children who have learned the Access Consciousness tools use them. They say, "Why would I want to live in the cesspool? If something works, I am going to use it." We adults tend to take a different approach. We want to examine everything carefully before we use it; we want to look at it from every angle. Rather than embrace the possibilities, we look for reasons to reject them.

How many possibilities do you reject in your life?

What if you were to choose the possibilities instead of rejecting the possibilities?

Your Kids Have Choice

It is not for you to worry whether your kids choose to be conscious or not; it is their life. They need to choose what works for them. Parents are what children rebel against in order to prove they can have their own life. Are they ever going to approve of you? No. They can't approve of you, because if they did, they wouldn't be able to have their own lives. You are the one they have to rebel against in order to know the life they are choosing is right for them. If you approved of their life, they would have to change it. Rebellion is the way they know they are choosing for them.

Most people believe they are choosing for them if they are choosing against somebody else. How much of your life have you chosen against others as though that was choosing for you? *Everything that is, times a godzillion will you destroy and uncreate it all, please? Thank you. Right and wrong, good and bad, POD and POC, all nine, shorts, boys and beyonds.*

Talking to Your Kids About Sex

Most people do not talk with their children about sex, and yet we recognize that people are sexual at an early age. What if you could talk truth about sex? Not what everybody tells you it ought to be: love, romance, living happily ever after and all that kind of thing, but where people are functioning from that isn't really functional.

My Dad gave me a book about sex and he said, "Read this book chapter by chapter and if you have any questions, ask me at the end of each chapter." I went away to a friend's house and I read the whole book in about a day and a half. My dad asked if I had read the book and I said, "Yep, I read the whole thing. " He asked if I had any questions for him, and I couldn't see that he knew anything more than I did at the time, so that was the end of our conversation about sex. The fact that he gave me a book was more than most kids get.

What are they teaching in school as sex education? Right now sex education in the schools is all about how if you have sex, you will get a sexually transmitted disease and probably die. Notice the emphasis on joy and nurturing and how great it is for your body? There's so much sexual dysfunction in this world right now that it is time to look at what is, and what we would like it to be, and then start to create that for ourselves.

How much of what you were taught about sex has worked really well for you so far? So would you consider getting rid of all the erroneous piles of debris you have learned about sex, relationship and copulation? *Everything that is times a godzillion, will you destroy and uncreate it all, please? Thank you. Right and wrong, good and bad, POD and POC, all nine, shorts, boys and beyonds.*

When kids are experiencing sexual energies and sexual desires, you can acknowledge what is there without having to do anything with it. If you don't have those conversations with them, they grow up thinking sex is dirty and wrong.

My daughter told me that her friend said to her, "Your dad is hot!"

I said, "Wow, thank you. Tell her I wish I were twenty years younger or that she was twenty years older, because that could be a possibility. What a sadness!" The friend got embarrassed and flustered but she was delighted. I just acknowledged that energy was there.

You can show kids about allowance by allowing them to receive these energies without judging them or making them significant. What if you could create your own reality about what sex can be rather than buying other people's points of view about it?

Empower Your Kids to Choose

As a parent, when you see your child doing something that is not in their best interests and you would like to see them make a different choice, you can present that different choice—but you can't be vested in the outcome. You may be aware of how there could be a different choice but you still have to be willing for it to turn out however it turns out. The only thing you can do is give your kids a sense of self so they can choose.

How can you give that to children if they grow up in an environment where you have divorced yourself in your relationship? They see that in you, and they start to divorce themselves too.

When you start standing up and being you, they will say, "Wait a minute, Mom (or Dad) is being different. I want to be more like that," and then they will choose it. You have got to choose the 990% of you so you can inspire your kids. You can't diminish you as a way of inspiring your kids or inviting them to a different possibility. When you say, "Sorry, this doesn't work for me; something else will have to happen," they will learn they can choose change too.

You need to function from total allowance and you have to be in allowance of your kids not changing. If you are aware that they will *not* change, usually they *will* change.

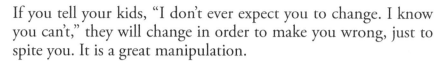

If you tell your kids, "I don't ever expect you to change. I know you can't," they will change in order to make you wrong, just to spite you. It is a great manipulation.

You will have less trauma and drama in your life because no matter what comes up, by being in allowance, it will change. You can just be the 990% of you, which is a totally different way to be. The 990% is the choice for being. When you are not divorcing you but actually being all of you, the doors to different things happening in your life start to open.

Family Relationships in the 990%

What would family relationships in the 990% look like? It would be the elimination and eradication of all relationships in the sense that all distance between you and everyone would go away. If the distance between you and everything and everyone went away, what would you have? You would have you and you would have total choice.

What does it look like to have total choice? It would be living in ten-second increments, which is: "You have ten seconds to live the rest of your life, what do you choose? Okay that lifetime is over. You have ten seconds to live the rest of your life, what do you choose?" That is total choice.

But we try to make our choices based on what somebody else is going to decide, think or do as a result of our choice. No! Choice is: "This is what I would like to choose. If you don't like it, okay. If you do like it, okay."

This is the country of 990%. It is a place you have never been—or you may have had momentary excursions there, but they have only been momentary because as soon as you realize you're out of the cesspool you say, "Wait, where are the rest of the turds? If I can't take all the turds with me, I'm not going to swim."

Have you been trying for years to make a relationship work that isn't working? Are you waiting in futility? If you're waiting for your kids to go along with you to the clear pool, you are waiting in futility. Your kids will make their choices just the way you do. You are not responsible for their choice even if they are your children.

How can you go to the clear pool without your children? Well, it is not a "how," it is a choice. What do you choose? Do you want to miss them or do you want to have them in your life? I don't miss my kids; they miss me. They say, "Dad, call me. Dad, why don't you hang out with me?"

I ask, "When would you like to hang out? What about tomorrow? What time would you like to hang out? How about in the morning? Should I call you or will you call me?"

They say, "You call me."

I say, "Okay." So I call for four hours and get no answer. Did they really want to hang out with me or did they just want me to commit to hanging out with them?

My daughter used to say, "I can't wait until you get home. I miss you so much!" I'd get home and she would say, "I'm going out with my friends. Do you mind?"

Of course I tell her I don't mind.

She says, "But I told you I missed you."

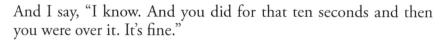

And I say, "I know. And you did for that ten seconds and then you were over it. It's fine."

If you are living in ten-second increments of choice then ten seconds of missing someone is no big deal. You just move on! You cannot make anything significant.

Tool: Don't Make It Significant

If you really want to get clear about the people in your life, look at your friends and family and make them into cartoon characters: Elmer Fudd, Bugs Bunny, Daffy Duck, Wile E. Coyote, the Roadrunner, Eeyore and so on. How serious are their traumas and dramas when you turn them into cartoon characters? It gets very hard to take anyone seriously when you see them as a cartoon character. This is a great tool for breaking apart the significance of relationship. If you have somebody who is significant in your life, try calling them your "insignificant other." Does it feel good to call them your insignificant other?

When you say "Hi, my insignificant other" to someone, they will usually cackle with laughter. They think it's funny. When you introduce somebody and you say, "This is my insignificant other" people say, "What?" Then you can say, "Yeah, this is just the guy I shag, but I love him a lot and he's really cute, don't you think? Would you like to try him?"

Would that change a few points of view? Oh yeah! That kind of thing makes people think and look from a different place. Sometimes it will even get them to ask a question that will open them up to a new awareness. Oh dear! That would be too bad!

Chapter Twenty-Four

CARING FOR OTHERS

What is the difference between *caring for* and *taking care of?* Do you feel the difference in the energy? When you take care of others, you do things for them; when you care for others, you allow them to be what they choose. True caring is the willingness to allow somebody to be exactly what they are choosing to be. Taking care of somebody is trying to change them into what will make them better. Which one is more expansive—taking care of or caring for? Caring for is the more expansive choice.

Caring as Abuse

My ex-wife's family screamed all the time; for her screaming meant you cared. She always wanted to fight and scream because that was her idea of caring. She grew up with two alcoholic parents who always fought and screamed at each other so our whole marriage was about fighting and screaming.

We went to her parent's house for Christmas one year and it was so beautiful. It was the first white Christmas I ever had. There was snowfall on Christmas morning and we were in a house that was built in 1860. It had a fireplace in every room and we had Yule logs burning in each one. It was perfect. Her parents joined us just before dinner and they started screaming at the top of their lungs at each other. That made me not want to go in and have a Christmas dinner with them, and from that point on it was downhill the rest of the night. However, some people like that. It is part of what they consider caring. If you grow up in a family where people scream at you and they say, "The only reason I do this is because I love you," you begin to believe that's true. Unfortunately most people think that you only abuse the ones you love.

How much abuse are you allowing in your life that you think proves the person loves you? *Everything that is, times a godzillion, will you destroy and uncreate it all, please? Thank you. Right and wrong, good and bad, POD and POC, all nine, shorts, boys and beyonds.*

Worrying About People

Was there somebody in your family who worried all the time? As a kid, you saw that person worrying and you thought, "If I could solve their worry, they could stop worrying. They wouldn't have to worry anymore and I wouldn't have to worry, and I don't need to worry—but how can I stop them worrying?" So you started taking on their worry in order to get them out of their worry, but that didn't work because they were probably taking the worry on from somebody else too.

From that point forward, you have picked people who had worry in their universe and you took on their worry. When you walk down the street and somebody's worrying, you take on their worry. Then you marry somebody who also had that worry reward system because you figure that if you could finally solve their worry then you would finally solve your issue around worry.

Do you feel exhausted already? Yes! This is what we all do, whether it's anger or worry or fear. Whatever it is, when you grow up with somebody who has that going on, you take that crap on, thinking you are solving their problem. You create relationships with people who are just like the person whose problem you couldn't solve. You figure if you solve it with them, you will solve it with the other person and then you won't have that to deal with anymore. It doesn't work. *They* have to change it, not you.

Get the energy of everything you have done to take on what you couldn't solve (which didn't solve anything) but makes you go into relationships with people you have to solve a problem with. *Everything that is, times a godzillion, will you destroy and uncreate it all, please? Thank you. Right and wrong, good and bad, POD and POC, all 9, shorts, boys and beyonds.*

You also try to make yourself responsible for anybody who has that energy or who functions from worry, anger, fear or whatever it is. As soon as you perceive it, you try to change it or take it on to make it different. You don't even have to know who the person is; it might be someone walking by. You may be picking it up from someone anywhere in the world.

Dain recalls a time when I was on the phone, trying to handle a problem with something. He was struck by the strength of the impulse that he had to do something to help. He caught himself wondering what he could do, how could he handle that problem, how could he change it? It wasn't a problem that had anything to do with him, yet he wondered how he could fold, bend, staple and mutilate himself to change this problem. Then he realized that all through his life, whenever anyone had a problem, he thought he was the one responsible for changing it. Do you have that point of view?

Were you the most responsible one in your family even when you were two years old because you were the one who was most aware in your family? Were you more responsible than your parents? Does that make you the one who is automatically responsible for solving everything?

You are trying to take care of someone and keep them safe by worrying about them. You have some conclusion in place that you have to do this. That makes it a creation; you created it, so you can uncreate it just as easily.

Would you like to give up that job now? *Everything that is times a godzillion, will you destroy and uncreate it all, please? Thank you. Right and wrong, good and bad, POD and POC, all nine, shorts, boys and beyonds.*

I once got a call from my daughter when she was in Boston. She said, "Dad, I feel really fearful, like somebody could be standing outside my house."

211

I said, "Okay, so close your eyes and point to where that's occurring. Is it close or is it several blocks away?"

She said, "Oh, its several blocks away."

So I asked, "Several blocks away is Main Street, right? Do you suppose a woman walking down Main Street is feeling fearful of those guys who hang out on the corners, because that's not a real nice neighborhood?"

My daughter instantly brightened up and said, "Oh, yeah!" and was able to go to sleep with no trouble. She recognized that it wasn't hers, and she no longer had to worry about it. She had been picking up another woman's point of view that she could be raped as she walked down the street.

Making People Happy

If you grew up with somebody who worried all the time, whenever anybody is worrying, you will pick it up and think it is yours. As I have said, before the age of two you don't see the separation between you and your parents so when they worry, you assume their worry is your worry. You try to take it away from them in order to make them feel better, but it doesn't work. Did you ever try to make your parents happy when you were a kid? Did it ever work? No. Why?

You never made them happy because they didn't want to be happy. They wanted to be sad. They wanted to worry; they wanted to be unhappy because being unhappy means your life is real. Have you ever noticed that if you are sad people say, "Oh, what's wrong, honey?" If you are happy they ask, "What drug are you on?" Why are you supposedly on a drug when you are happy?

Happiness is definitely a bad thing in this world. It's bizarre. You are obviously not serious enough if you smile and laugh too much!

Chapter Twenty-Five

GETTING TO KNOW YOUR BODY

We would like you to aim for a sense of communion with your body where you have no judgment of it and you are willing to hear it. When you have this kind of relationship with your body, you are willing to ask it questions and receive the information it gives to you.

I Don't Like My Body

Most people don't like their body. They see it as a source of un-consciousness; they will go out and do drugs and party hard in order to turn off their awareness so they can make sure they are like other people. The majority of unconsciousness and anti-consciousness occurs as a result of people's idea that their body is not a perfect vehicle for them—that it is "less than." Every church, cult and religion defines your body as less than you, the soul or the being. Is any of that true or real? Or is that the party of unconsciousness that keeps you from having a body that works beautifully?

Is your body so separate from you that you have no communication with it? Or does it seem that all you feel through it is pain? Or that all you get from it is grief? Or that you have to get old or ugly or something other than what you'd really like to be?

Do you see your body as the perfect sex toy? No! Nobody does. No one looks at their body and says, "Wow, I came in with a perfect sex toy. I think I'll put it on the shelf and let it sit there. Twenty-five years from now I'll be so glad I didn't use it!"

Have you ever seen pictures of you from ten, fifteen or twenty years ago when you were judging you and your body harshly? Did you think you were ugly and awful then? And do you look at those pictures now and say, "Wow, I wish I could look as gorgeous now as I was then!" Do you get that you are still judging you and your body now in the same way? Would you be willing to change that?

What Does Judging Your Body Create?

You create your body with your judgment. When you judge it as too big, too small, too frumpy, too saggy, too ugly, too old, too young, or whatever it is, the judgment creates more of that, not less. Your body creates what you judge it to be. Isn't that cool?

It's kind of like when somebody tells you that you are stupid all the time. Do you get smarter? Or do you start feeling more and more stupid? Whereas if someone was to ask you, "Hey, would you consider the possibility of doing it this way?" that would invite you to a different possibility. The same thing is true with your body. You will get what you desire if you are willing to ask a question. "Hey body, what would it take to change this?" Instead most of us go into a litany of judgment as though that's going to make it better.

Everything you have done to decide the litany of judgment will make your body better or your life better or your relationship better, or anything else better, *will you destroy and uncreate it, please? Thank you. Right and wrong, good and bad, POD and POC, all nine, shorts, boys and beyonds.*

I don't know if you're aware of this, but telling people what they've done wrong usually doesn't get them to change. You think, "Let me tell my kid what he did wrong and maybe he'll change it." It doesn't usually work that way when it's done from a place of judgment. Of course, that will also apply to husbands, wives, girlfriends, boyfriends, friends, every relationship you have, including your relationship with your body.

What Are You Telling Your Body?

Have you ever noticed that whatever you focus on is all you can see? When you are a teenager and you have a zit, the only thing you will see in the mirror is the zit. You never see anything else. If you think your lips are too skinny, you focus on how your lips are too skinny. If you think your body is too saggy or too fat or too anything, that will be all you can see, no matter what. You don't realize that other people see it differently.

How much time do you spend judging you? When you get up in the morning do you look in the mirror and say, "Wow, I am cool, I am beautiful, look at how amazing I am," or do you say, "Oh my God! Look at how saggy, draggy and old I am?" You are looking at your body with total judgment, you are creating it from total judgment and you never see what is. You only see what you judge.

Dain used to work out at a gym, and he would watch guys doing their bodybuilding stuff. They would have almost perfect bodies yet they would be in total judgment of them. Nothing was right, nothing was perfect, nothing was good. They looked at their bodies with total judgment. Guess what their body created for them in the mirror? The image of what they judged. What if you were willing to look at your body without judgment? What would it actually appear to be?

Everything you have done to always look through the eyes of judgment, never the eyes of truth, awareness or possibility; *everything that is, times a godzillion will you destroy and uncreate it all, please? Thank you. Right and wrong, good and bad, POD and POC, all nine, shorts, boys and beyonds.*

The Perfect Body

Perfect is a judgment. You have an idea of what your perfect body should be but you never see the body that you have as perfect. You have to love your body for what it is, not what you think it ought to be. Where do we come up with the standards for what our body should be, anyway? People come up with statements like, "You're supposed to be tall, thin and blonde." You buy all kinds of bizarre points of view about what your body is supposed to look like.

Your body has a point of view about what it would like to look like. Is your body happy with the way it looks? We take a point of view of what our bodies should look like but we never ask, "Body, what do you want to look like? You may not be happy with the way it looks, but it may be perfectly happy—or it may want to look like something different. We always assume we have control over our body and the way we get control is by judging it out of existence. Every judgment you use against your body is a way to separate from it.

Nobody judges your body the way you do. Other people only judge it because you have a sign up that says "kick me here." Every judgment creates a little sign somewhere on your body that says, "This is what I judge about me. Look at this, talk about this, judge me this way." It is like a big flashing sign that everybody sees and then they say, "You're looking a bit old and tired today." How did they know you were feeling old and tired today? It must be true! No, you were judging that you looked old and tired, so guess what they say? You are looking old and tired. That makes your judgment right—and what is more important than anything else? Being right. You would rather be right than be free.

Poor body! It likes you more than you like it. Your body is really your best friend. It's like having a puppy. You know how puppies are just there for you? They are always willing to do whatever you want? Your puppy knows that when you kick it, you didn't really mean it and it comes over to lick you because you must be having a bad day and it wants to make you feel better. So, how many times a day do you kick your body?

Your body actually has consciousness and awareness of its own, but you treat it as if it is an unaware, retarded stepchild that you

218

need to control in order to get anything done. Your body actually has a tremendous amount of awareness it can share with you if you start asking it about the things that concern it. "Body, what would you like to eat? Body, will this be nurturing to you? Body, would you like to have sex with this person? Your body will actually communicate with you if you ask it a question.

Your Body Gives You Information

Your body is a sensory organ. It is designed to give you information. When you "feel" energies that don't "feel good," you can ask your body, "Okay body, what are you trying to tell me?" You have probably felt energies your whole life that have nothing to do with you; you assume they are yours and lock them into your body.

Let's say you grew up in a family where somebody was incredibly angry but never expressed it. You would have been aware of that energy even if you did not cognitively understand what you were aware of. You interpreted that awareness as an energy that was part of you. What do you do now? You pick up other people's anger and assume it is yours. If you can experience it, feel it or perceive it, you assume it must be your anger. This is not necessarily true. Ask your body, "What are you really experiencing here? What are you really feeling? What is this that I am really perceiving in my body?"

It is important to realize your body is trying to tell you things all the time. You say, "Oh, I feel bad, oh, that hurts, oh, I feel like shit." What question is that? Notice there's no question in that at all?

Most of the time your body is telling you about what's going on in someone else's body or about some other energy that you have no other way of getting the information about. Your body is like a cat's whiskers; its job is to give you information, but if you don't ask the question, you don't ever get the information.

When Dain was practicing as a chiropractor, a guy came in with lower back pain. Dain did adjustments with the guy for three months, and nothing would change. It would get better and then get worse, get better and get worse. One day Dain asked the guy, "So, is this pain yours or someone else's?"

The patient said, "Wow. It's someone else's."

Dain asked, "How does it feel now?"

The patient said, "Fifty percent better!"

It wasn't actually his in the first place. His body was giving him the information about what was going on with other people around him, and once he acknowledged that, his body didn't have to create the pain anymore.

Your Body Can Help You

When you get to the point where you can have a sense of communion with your body and you ask it what it needs, all kinds of strange things can show up.

At one time I noticed that my joints were hurting so I went to an endocrinologist for an examination. The doctor said that my growth hormones had quit and I had the body chemistry of an eighty-one-year-old man. I asked what was required to change that, and the doctor told me I had to take growth hormones for the rest of my life. So for three months I gave myself injections of growth hormones. Then one day, every time I went to stick the syringe in my leg, my body would move. I could not get a needle into it to save my life.

I asked, "Body, what you are trying to tell me? Do you want to take this stuff?"

"No!"

"Do you need anymore?"

"No!"

"Well, how are we going to get the growth hormone?"

"I'll make it!"

"Okay, fine."

I have not had an ache or pain in my joints since then. I just keep asking it for more growth hormones and my body has continued to generate them.

Your Body Reflects Your Point of View

Our bodies are amazing instruments that can facilitate us if we ask, but we usually don't bother to ask. We decide we are getting older and we don't ask, "What would it take to change this?" Your body is an exact reflection of your point of view about you. If you change your point of view, your reflection will change. What if you were grateful for your body? What might that look like for you and your body?

At one point I was looking at my body and I realized I had always wanted it to be slim and buff with great muscle structure. This is what I had decided and judged was the perfect body. However, the only buff I got was a big gut, because my body could only do bulk; it couldn't do buff. I said, "Okay, body, what would you like to look like?" About three months went by and one day I was watching TV and I saw a skinny, tall body that was buff and lean. It was a swimmer's kind of body. I got that this was the body shape my body desired to have. I looked at it and said, "Are you kidding? You want to look like that? There's no way! Our hips are too wide; there's no way that is going to happen!"

However, I made the choice to do whatever it took to create my body like that. I was willing to do whatever my body asked me to do. About two weeks later I was at the beach throwing a Frisbee and all of a sudden my hips went crack-crack-crack! I said, "Whoa! What just happened? That hurt!" I lost two inches in my hips and waist. That is not supposed to be possible.

Your body knows what to do if you will ask it to show you. We just don't ask. My body asked me to go play Frisbee. I went and played Frisbee and suddenly my hips and waist were narrower, and I have since shed a lot of weight. It's weird but it works.

Your Body Will Tell You What It Requires

Please start listening to your body. Become willing to receive all of its awareness and information; your body will tell you what it wants. You can even ask it what it would like to wear each day, because it wears the clothes, you don't. You, the being, don't wear anything. Your body is far more phenomenal than you think it is.

I met a guy who did lasers, supplements, muscle testing and all kinds of weird stuff and he was really good at what he did. I asked my body if it would be rewarding to see him and got a yes so I went and had a session. The guy recommended supplements and I asked, "Body, do you want these?" I got a *yes,* so I was willing to take the supplements to the extent my body wanted them. Normally I wouldn't buy supplements, but I don't say, "I have to do everything with energy work" and I am not willing to cut off the awareness of what my body is asking for.

You have to allow people to have their point of view and allow you to have yours. When you are told you have to ingest this or take that, you have to ask, "Is it really true that I need to do this? That doesn't make me feel light so that's a lie." The guy who sold the supplements wanted to sell me bucket loads of supplements. I would ask, "Body, do you want this? How many do you want?" And I would follow the *yes* or *no* my body gave me.

Ninety percent of the problems we have with our bodies stem from the fact that we don't listen to what they tell us. Have you ever gone to bed with somebody you knew you shouldn't have gone to bed with, but you went anyway? We can override our bodies. How often do we do that? How often have you overridden what your body was trying to tell you? Way more than you should have? Way less than you should have? Or so often that your poor body feels like it has been dishonored in totality?

Avoiding Pain

Your body likes to move. That is what it is designed to do, however there are a lot of people who desperately try to exercise and they work their body until it hurts. If you look at *moving* your body rather than *exercising* it, your body will be more supple, open and available and you will start to have some fun with it. Ask your body, "What kind of movement would you like today?"

"No pain no gain" is one of the biggest lies you buy with regard to changing your body. If you want to change something it should be done with ease, joy and glory—like the rest of your life.

Pain is neither a necessity nor a reality. Pain is a creation. It is a point of view you take. When my kids were little they would fall down and hit the pavement. I would walk over and ask, "Did you break the cement?" They would look at the ground and see it was all okay and with great relief, they would say, "No!" Then they would get up and run away happy. They would never get a bump on their head. Other parents would see their kid fall and they would say, "Oh my God! Are you okay?" Their kids would cry and get a big bump and a bruise on their head. My kids never had bruises. What's the difference? Their point of view.

Your point of view creates your reality. It is not the other way around. Why can people walk over hot coals and it doesn't blister and it doesn't hurt? Because pain is not real. It is a creation, not a truth.

Do you live your life from the point of view of trying to avoid pain? People say, "You hurt me when you said that." Really? How is that possible? You can say the same thing to another person and it doesn't hurt them at all because they don't consider it painful. But if you say something to someone and they decide it's painful, it will be painful. So which creates pain? Your decision or the truth?

Tool: Make It Infinite

This tool will help you separate the truth from the lies. When you use this tool, you can see what is going on for what it truly is and not what you have decided it is. If you make something infinite that is a lie, it will disappear. Anything that is true will become more substantial.

Exercise: *Think about somebody you have an upset with. Get all those feelings and make them infinite, bigger than the universe. Do they disappear or become more substantial? They disappear, right? That's because what is occurring is different than what you believe it is.*

Now think about somebody you care about. Get all those feelings and make them infinite, bigger than the universe. Do they become more substantial? Maybe you care more than you want to admit to yourself.

You are an infinite being and you are going to feel things. It is okay. Just make them infinite, bigger than the universe, and they will start to disappear and you will not have to be the effect of them. When you come too close to your body, you feel things and you begin to pull them into your body, which is not in your best interest. You make things real, intense and dense when you don't expand out. When you are contracted and you get the awareness of all that energy, there will seem to be a lot of it and very little of you to dissipate it.

You receive information all the time and if you just make it infinite, bigger than the universe, the part of it that is a lie goes away and the part of it you need to deal with remains. That is the only part you get to deal with and take care of. Dealing with it begins with asking, "What is this? Am I required to do anything with it? What can I be or do to facilitate change here?"

When you perceive something that is going on for someone and you try to take it away from them, you are not changing anything. They are probably trying to take it away from somebody else—and when you take it away from them, you are just moving it around in some kind of circle. It is not going to go away until you are willing to ask, "Can we now stop?"

For example, say you are aware of a pain in someone's body. There are some questions you can ask: "Is it their pain? Is their body trying to tell them something? Are they actually experiencing it as a pain—or have they numbed themselves out so much they can't pay attention to their body?" Ask the question and if it makes you feel lighter, it is a yes, and if it makes you feel heavy, it is a no. Simple as that. You are not looking for answers.

Sometimes when somebody has a pain you feel it in your body because you know their body is screaming at your body, "Fix me!" In that situation you can just put your hand on their shoulder or back, or even shake hands and hold it just a little bit longer than is comfortable for them and in so doing you can take the pain out of their body. Do this because it makes your life easier, not because you want to "help" others. Be aware that as long as their body is in pain, yours will scream, so make it easier on yourself. This is learning to use your awareness instead of trying to get rid of it.

What Can Your Body Tell You About Food?

You can ask your body, "Do you want to eat? Or do you want something to drink?" Then ask your body to show you what it would like.

When you are eating what your body wants, it will feel good and taste good. If it tastes good, you know you've got the right thing. If you ask your body questions and play with this, you can begin to develop a different relationship with your body. You may not get a clear answer at first and you may miss a lot to begin with, but then you will begin to see that when you get it, it will feel a certain way. You will know that every time it feels that way, you are getting what your body actually wants.

As you begin to ask your body what it wants, it may desire the strangest things—but they will taste good! It might ask for Corona beer and popcorn for dinner. It may ask for champagne and sweet pie and that's all. Would you be willing to have just wine, cheese, salami and fruit for dinner if that is what your body desires?

For most of us, our bodies don't desire very much in the way of food. The American portion size is about four times what any person needs to eat. It is way too much food. Be willing to leave a plate of food uneaten. If you don't waste it, you will waist it.

When you feed your body are you nurturing it or killing it? We believe we are nurturing it but in truth, ingesting food your body does not require or desire actually kills it. Are you aware that the "energy" you get from 60-90% of the food you eat is used to break down and digest the food you are eating? So eating more does not give your body more energy; it uses more!

This is why you need to ask your body what it would like to eat. There is an amount of food and drink your body would like to have that actually facilitates it. What if food was a homeopathic for generating your body and not a source of energy for your body?

Science tells us that there is enough energy in the mitochondrial cells of each of our bodies to run a large city for three months, yet we act like we have no energy because we haven't eaten for a few hours. Where have we bought the idea that we need food for energy?

Here is an exercise you can do with your body. Ask it, "What would you like to eat that would access the energy you have available?" and see what starts to happen. What if you asked your body what it would take for it to have even more energy than you think it needs?

I asked my body what it would have to ingest in order to make it look ten years younger and it said, "Watermelon." So I ate watermelon for almost three weeks until one day my body didn't want to eat watermelon anymore. At the end of that time I looked about ten years younger. Watermelon was a homeopathic for undoing the aging process for my body.

Would you like to have that kind of relationship with your body?

Is Your Body Feeling Tired?

Do you often feel tired? How many times have you decided you are tired because you worked hard? How much of that is a truth and how much of it is a lie? The truth is that the energy you put into making yourself do things that bore you is what makes you feel tired. Have you noticed that you have to expend more energy to do the things you don't want to do?

You spend eight to ten times more energy to do things that bore you than you spend to do things you enjoy. You have to use eight to ten times the amount of energy normally required to do something that you resist doing, and it will take anywhere from five to ten times longer to do it.

How much of your life are you forcing yourself to do things you don't actually like to do? *Everything that brought up will you destroy and uncreate it all, please? Yes? Thank you. Right and wrong, good and bad, POD and POC, all nine, shorts, boys and beyonds.*

Do You Think You Are Getting Old?

The Bible talks about people living to be 900 years old, so why is it that we only live to be around 80 years old?

Try this exercise. *Ask your body how long it would like to live. You have to ask your body, not you. Trust the energy and choose what feels light.*

Would your body like to live to be more than 100 years old or less than 100 years old? More!

Would your body like to live for more than 300 years or less than 300 years? More!

More than 500 years or less than 500 years? More!

Would your body like to be more than 800 years old or less than 800 years old? More!

Please notice that your body would be willing to live 800 years or more but you won't let it live to be more than 100 years old.

You assume that being 800 years old means you will look like Methuselah with wrinkles from head to toe. What if that is not the case? We don't have to have that as reality, yet we all believe that we will get old and wrinkly and sick. Why? Because we have decided that "age" is real. We do birthday parties and celebrate getting older. We are sure that when we get to be 60-plus years old we will be pathetic and old. Your point of view creates your reality, so would you be willing to give up celebrating your birthday as significant and give up buying into the lie of aging as real?

Would an infinite being create a body that would function as finite? No. An infinite being would create a body that had infinite capacity. If your body has the capacity to live 800 years and it is not, would it make sense that you are doing something to it that stops it from being able to live that long? What do you suppose that something might be? Judgment.

When did you stop strutting? When did you give it up? What age are you defining yourself as that your body is not happy with? The answer is just about any age you are currently defining yourself as. What if you didn't have to look any older than you do today for the next ten years? Would that be of any value to you? When you are willing to change your point of view, you can change what shows up in your body.

At what age did you turn your body off? Look at that age and ask, "What decision, judgment, conclusion or computation did I use there?" There will be a sense of wrongness, which is like a fixed conclusion, but there's a decision there too. There is a decision you have made about the wrongness of your body.

When kids are young, they are just sexual. They don't have a point of view about it. As they get older, they learn that it's wrong to do those things. Then when they're teenagers, someone tells them they're ugly or they're bad or they're fat, and they begin to reject the sensations and awareness in their body, and they start to turn their body off in order to be okay about being rejected.

Everything you have done to turn you and your body off, everything you have done to turn your choice for living off in favor of anybody else's point of view, *will you destroy and uncreate all that?*

Yes? Thank you. Right and wrong, good and bad, POD and POC, all nine, shorts, boys and beyonds.

If you are going to live to be 800 years old, you have to be willing to have a life that is different from the one you have been currently creating. Why would you want to live the limited life you have for another 750 plus years?

Eliminating Sexual Energy from Your Body

Are you trying to get to God through no sex? That's called piety and purity. What if you were willing to be as demented and depraved as you truly are? Do you tend to deprive yourself so no one will know that you're actually depraved?

Consciousness has to do with infinite choice. The spiritual point of view is that you have to overcome the limitations of the flesh in order to have the divine lightness and the love that will take you to God. How many gods have you worshiped in all your lifetimes? Have any of them ever answered your prayers? Did you know you are the god of your own reality? The one thing about most churches, cults and religions is they eliminate sexual energy as a part of life. How does your body feel about eliminating sexual energy?

The Dalai Lama and all the monks have the point of view that if you eliminate the desire for sex, you eliminate the need of the flesh, as though the flesh is a need. What if the flesh wasn't a need? What if it was a choice—and the choice made a creative energy in your body? The truth is that sexual energy is generative energy. Why would you eliminate that from your body?

231

People who start to age dynamically have eliminated sexual energy from their life. They start to look bad, they start to feel bad and they start feel pain and all kinds of other things. The growth hormones that your body is supposed to have are based on the sexual energy of your body. The growth hormones continue to expand as long as you're willing to have sexual energy. As soon as you turn off the sexual energy, you turn off your growth hormones. The growth hormones are what keep the body from aging dynamically.

Having sexual energy does not mean you have to copulate all the time. You always have choice of whether you copulate or not. You don't have to be on or off. What if your body was turned on all the time?

How much energy do you use against your body to turn off the sexual energy? A lot, a little, or megatons? *Everything that is, will you destroy and uncreate it all? Yes? Thank you. Right and wrong, good and bad, POD and POC, all nine, shorts, boys and beyonds.*

The Joy of Embodiment

Embodiment is not just about your body. It is about this whole reality. If you are willing to receive this whole reality, then a different kind of embodiment can occur for you. There's a sense of joy and peace that comes with it. You can watch people choosing whatever they choose and know that there is oneness, and in oneness all things are included and nothing is judged. You won't have a judgment that death is wrong and you won't have a judgment that what anybody chooses is a wrongness.

Chapter Twenty-Six

SECRETS TO GREAT SEX

In this discussion, it is helpful to make the distinction between sex, sexuality and copulation. Sex is where you are walking tall, feeling good and strutting your stuff. *Sexuality* is a judgment and a definition of you based on your sexual preferences. *Copulation* is where you put the body parts together. Your body has sex, not you, so the first place to start is by looking at what your body would like to have as nurturing copulation.

What Would Your Body Like?

I have always picked the demon bitch from hell as a partner. Of course, it never turned out well. All I had to do was see a woman who was a demon bitch from hell and I would say, "Oh my God, she's so beautiful. I love her. She's so wonderful; she's so attractive. Can I have her?" Yes, I could have her, provided I was willing to sell my soul to the devil.

One day I finally asked my body to show me what would be nurturing for it in copulation.

Shortly after that I was at a swap meet and as I walked around the marketplace I asked, "Body, show me what kind of person you would be attracted to. What kind of body would be nurturing to you in copulation?"

All of a sudden I felt a tug. I turned around and there was the ugliest woman I had ever seen. I said, "Okay, fine, you want to sleep with ugly people." I went on a little further and felt another tug and there was a gay man. I thought, "That's strange. I didn't know we were gay, but okay, fine. Ugly, gay people is what we need." A little further on there was an old woman with a walker and I got another tug. I thought, "Okay, this is just weird. Ugly, gay, geriatric!" The next tug I got was from a little kid and by then I was totally confused. Ugly, gay, geriatric pedophile? What are you talking about body? Suddenly I realized all four of those bodies had a similar vibration, and I was aware that this was the kind of energy that would be nurturing to me. It was not the demon bitch from hell that I had always chosen. It was this particular energy that would be nurturing to me. Now I know to look for that energy in somebody I choose to have sex with.

What Will Having Sex with You Create?

Once you become aware of the energy that would be nurturing for your body, you can be attracted to somebody, realize that you might like to have sex with them and then ask, "Okay body, is this going to be nurturing to you?" If it isn't, don't go there.

Here is a question you can use: "How will this turn out in six months, nine months, or a year into the future?"

Be aware of what you are choosing and what that will create in your life. You are an infinite being; you have the ability to know what your choices are going to create. This information is helpful if you are willing to have it, but a lot of people aren't willing, because they would rather get laid. Or they have the idea that everything will turn out just fine.

Have you ever started an affair because you thought it would be fun? And then it turned out to be something that wasn't fun? Did you see the movie *Fatal Attraction?* If you are one of those people who has the point of view that you would rather get laid or you know everything is going to turn out just fine, even though it never has before, you might want see that movie.

Dain says that before he discovered this tool, he wasn't willing to look at the likely result of having sex with somebody. He wanted to believe he could do it and have the joy of sex he knew was possible. What you know is possible is irrelevant. You have to look at what the other person has decided is real, because what they have decided is real will trump what you have decided is possible every single time.

It is simple to access this information. The energy that will be created is the energy that comes up the moment you think about going there. As soon as you contemplate anything, whether it is having sex with somebody, having an affair with somebody, buying a car, buying a house, or anything else, the energy that comes up will match the energy that will get created in your life if you choose to do it. It is that simple, but nobody has ever told you that. Nobody has ever told you that the energy that comes up is your awareness kicking in to tell you what's going to happen.

Choice creates awareness. You are aware instantaneously. You look at doing something and instantaneously you become aware. At that moment, do you choose to acknowledge and honor your awareness or do you choose to cut it off and divorce another of piece of you?

When you consider copulating with somebody and you are willing ask, "Will this be expansive for me and my body?" oftentimes the answer is *no*. There are a lot of men who do not like women but have sex with them anyway, and there are a lot of women who don't like men but have sex with them as well. If you don't like them, why would you have sex with them?

Another point to be aware of with regards to sex is that if you decide, "This is the best sex I ever had," you will never get sex better than that in the future. That decision keeps you from having anything greater from that very moment on.

Would you like to give that up in favor of the possibility that there might be something that is even better than what you have already experienced? Yes? Everything that is, times a godzillion, will you destroy and uncreate it all, please? Thank you. *Right and wrong, good and bad, POD and POC, all nine, shorts, boys and beyonds.*

Conflicting Messages About Sex

Little kids are highly sexual until they are about eight years old when they are told, "If you touch that thing in public again, I'll cut your hand off." When you are a little boy, holding onto your handle is one of the greatest joys in life, but people slap you and say, "Don't do that! Bad boy! Nasty boy!"

Little girls are told, "If you do that again you are going to go to hell. You are going to grow warts." People say all kinds of weird stuff to you, and then you get to be eighteen and you are supposed to be a sexy thing and they are still saying, "Don't let anybody touch it." Then you get married and you are supposed to let your partner touch it and enjoy the hell out of it. Does that create any conflictual universes?

How many conflictual universes, paradigms and realities do you have about what is appropriate sexually and what is not appropriate sexually—none of which has anything to do with sanity? *Everything that is, times a godzillion, will you destroy and uncreate it all, please? Thank you. Right and wrong, good and bad, POD and POC, all nine, shorts, boys and beyonds.*

Opposing View of Sex and Relationship

Most women do copulation in order to create a relationship and most men do relationship in order to create copulation. Does that create a little conflict between the sexes? Just a tad! Please be willing to consider this and look at the person you are with. If you are a woman, look at the man and ask energetically, "Is he willing to do relationship in order to copulate? Yes? No?" Follow the energy. You are looking for what feels light. If the light answer is yes then ask yourself if you will be happy with just copulating. Is that enough for you?

You can also ask, "Am I willing to do copulation in order to get this relationship? Will that work for me?" If it works for you, no problem. This is about having what you desire and seeing whether it is going to work for you. It is not about seeing if you can fit your choices into the box of what you are supposed to have based on what everybody in contextual reality tells you that you must have.

If you are a man and you are doing relationship to get copulation, you may want to ask, "Is this going to be enough for me?" If it is, okay cool. Whether you are a woman or a man, wouldn't you prefer to love the person you are with rather than the person you want them to be?

How many fixed points of view have you taken on from others about what relationship is supposed to be? And how many points of view have you taken from others about what copulation is supposed to be? *Everything that is, times a godzillion, will you destroy and uncreate it all, please? Thank you. Right and wrong, good and bad, POD and POC, all nine, shorts, boys and beyonds.*

Choosing Men Who Hate Women

There are a whole lot of women who do not like men and there are a whole lot of men who do not like women. And a lot of women choose men who don't like women because they find them extremely exciting. They think somebody who actually likes women is boring. There's no challenge with a man who likes women. Yes, there's no challenge, but there is a whole lot more great sex possible!

That's the reason you have to ask, "Will this be a contribution to my life or not?" Remember to ask that and make sure to have "someone who actually likes the sex I am" on your list of things you want in a relationship. If you are a female, ask for a man who likes females, not a man who doesn't!

Judgment Is Not a Turn On

Towards the end of my marriage, I could not enjoy sex with my ex-wife because every time she would reach for me, my body would withdraw. Every morning she would deliver a litany of judgment at my body. She said things like, "I can't believe you are so flabby; you need to go work out. I can't believe you are so fat; you need to get skinnier. I can't believe you are so skinny; you need to get fatter, I can't believe you are so wrinkled; you need to do something about that." I started to sleep on the far edge of the bed because my body was on edge all the time. I didn't understand why that was occurring until I finally realized I had been living in a constant state of judgment of my body. She had done so much judgment of my body that it didn't want to be touched.

Everywhere you have done judgment of your lover, every judgment you have projected or expected on them, everything you have thrown at them, everything you have delivered at them, let's erase and destroy and uncreate it all, across all time, space, dimensions and realities. *Everything that is, times a godzillion will you destroy and uncreate it all, please? Thank you. Right and wrong, good and bad, POD and POC, all nine, shorts, boys and beyonds.*

239

If you are attracted to someone because you believe you can change or improve them, you are looking for a diamond in the rough. Many women choose men that are diamonds in the rough. They have the point of view that if they can fix this guy up, he will be perfect! Then they polish him up and some other woman who likes him the way he is takes him.

Bringing Sex Back into Your Relationship

One woman we worked with had been refusing sex with her husband and she wanted to repair the relationship. She had made some overtures and he had said to her, "How can you just turn it on and off like that?" She tried to explain to him that she had made a decision to change, but it just made everything worse. So we gave her this tool.

Never tell people the truth, especially to somebody who is your lover. **Only tell people what they can hear** or they will throw what you have said back at you with daggers attached.

She went back to him, wearing his favorite perfume, and said, "I don't know what has changed. All of a sudden I realized that I have been missing what is so amazing about you." She made sure to wear something with a little cleavage, nothing extreme, just something simple and black that could get to the floor fast.

Tips for Turning Your Lover On

In a relationship where there has been no sex for a long time, you can start by saying, "Honey, can I give you a little massage? Let me rub your neck." Then say something like, "Wow, doing this is having an amazing effect. I'm starting to get turned on touching your body." Keep up with gentle massage and ask, "So how does that feel to you, lover? You know what, I sort of lost what an amazing turn-on you were. I'm glad it is starting to come back. Are you enjoying it?" This works for men and women.

Ladies, another thing you can do when you are out with your man is point out some women and ask, "Do you find that girl attractive? Would you consider sleeping with her? What kind of woman turns you on, darling? Would you consider sleeping with that one? What about that one?" If you do this while you walk down the street, you will encourage your man to think about sex. When you get home, he will be ready to go and he will want you. You may think I'm kidding, but it really works. The women who have used this tool find it works well and its fun! Are you willing to have fun with sex?

Tool: Enjoy the Manipulation

Many men protest about being manipulated, but actually every man will, if you really push him, admit that he likes it. We have done several sex and relationship classes where we have taught the men and the women what to say and even though both the husband and wife know that they are doing manipulation, they laugh and giggle and have more fun. They are grateful for it.

For the Guys: A man should always take a woman in his arms at least once a day and say, "Darling, I know that because you are in my life everything will work out well. I'm so grateful for you, I'm so grateful I have you in my life." Take notice, guys. If you put your arms around a woman and say that, she will be yours.

For the Girls: A woman has to put her arms around her husband and say, "Lover, will you do this for me?" and he will say, "Yeah honey, what do you want me to do?" Always. When you call a man *lover* or *sexy*, he will do what you ask twice as fast, and he will become joyful and playful with you. And then after he does three or four he-man tasks for you say, "Lover, would you consider coming to the bedroom with me?"

Call your man by his job title. When you call him *honey* or *sweetie*, he will feel like a little boy and will start to become less potent, which means you lose your stud in the bedroom. Call him lover and it's a guarantee that his voice will drop down deeper and he will say, "Sure honey, I'll do anything you want." It works every time.

All men feel like studs if you ask them to do something for you, so if he isn't your lover, you can say, for example, "Stud muffin, will you take this stuff to my car for me?" You've got to get that this actually works. So use it, it's a tool. It's miraculous.

Using Your Assets

Women, you have the one treasure every man is looking for—the golden vagina. Men will get down and bow to it. Women come in with an advantage over all men. They have cleavage and they have the golden vagina and they can get any man they want by using them, but they have to be willing to use them properly.

Properly does not mean being puritanical. *Properly* means recognizing you have an asset. People tend to create an asset and liability column by saying, "This is good about me; this is not good about me." Unfortunately you put the fact that you have breasts and a golden vagina in the liability column rather than the asset column. You try to make your personality, your hair, your face, your eyes, the way you dress, all of those things more valuable, and you put those in the asset column. If you recognize that breasts and a golden vagina are assets, you can have any man flat on his back in thirty seconds if you want him.

Be willing to manipulate, dominate and control the way you truly are. Humanoid women are dominatrixes. Not in the sense of beating their man—but occasionally tying them up and blindfolding them is not a bad idea. If you're a guy reading this, you are laughing aren't you? You're saying, "Yes, please, can I have one of those?" This is the truth about men. We would love to tell you that we men are smarter than that, but we would be lying.

Girls, if you are willing to show the right kind of cleavage and use the right kind of golden vagina, your man will never choose another woman. The problem with men is they are stupidly loyal. If they are getting sex with you, they will do whatever they can to make sure they get sex with you. You keep assuming they will go out and look for somebody else. No. Men are like stallions, all you have to do is tease them. Every woman who has had the courage to wind their man up has ended up owning that man totally.

Try these things out. The worst that will happen is you will lose the person you have to somebody else, and the best that will happen is you will get the information about what will actually work and you will own him.

Sex That Lasts All Night Long

There is a difference between copulation as an expansiveness and copulation as a contraction. Most people get off through the fight or flight syndrome, which is about pumping adrenaline in order to get off. When you are with somebody who pumps adrenaline to get off, you will also pump adrenaline to get off and in so doing you will exhaust your body and fall asleep. When you are with somebody who does copulation from a sense of expansiveness, then the energy of sex and copulation is generative and it makes you more awake, not less.

When you function from that generative energy, you can copulate all night, get up and work all day, copulate all night, get up and work all day, copulate all night and maybe get two hours of sleep each night for six, eight or ten days in a row and still have a huge amount of energy and possibility available. That is what occurs when you take on an expansive point of view. When you do sex from the contraction of orgasm based on adrenaline, which is a contractive state, all you can do is fall asleep.

This is the thing that most women object to, because most men have learned about sex from watching porn. How many women like to watch porn? Not many. Porn is mostly about force, violence and creating adrenaline in order to create the ejaculation and orgasm. And in creating more adrenaline, they fall asleep instantaneously after sex because there is no generative energy present.

Can I make a suggestion? Please read *Sex is Not a Four Letter Word But Relationship Oftentimes Is*. If you would like your partner to read it, leave it in the bathroom by mistake. Page 69 is where I begin talking about how to give your partner a full body orgasm. Besides that, it also gives you the tools for a nurturing, caring, intimate, trusting relationship.

Please Just Hold Me

Women are generally more relaxed and usually just want to be held, which they think is wonderful. That is nurturing for them. It's what they learned from papa; it is the feeling of being held and him saying, "I love you. I'll take care of you." Girls want that, and the guys think, "How come I'm not getting sex?" Unfortunately men are a little one-tracked. They don't do well with just sleeping with you. If you want to get rid of a man, sleep with him but don't have sex with him. If you want to keep him, give him oral sex and you've got him for at least fifteen days, just on the anticipation that he might get more.

When a woman copulates with a man, he feels honored, nurtured, cared for. He feels like he is a man. Whether it is oral sex or any form of copulation, his view is, "This woman is receiving me as the man that I am. She values me."

When a man is willing to hold a woman, she thinks, "He loves me for the woman I am." That is true; he does value you, but if you are not acknowledging and valuing him as the man he is as well, where does he fit in the computation? It is enormously helpful if you are both willing to see this and become aware of where each of you is functioning so you can create your relationship in a way that actually works for you.

The important thing is how you make it work for you. It is not about a right or wrong point of view. It is about "How do I make this work for me? What do I really want from this man or woman?"

The One Night Stand

Most people say, "The first time was so great, the second time will be better." How many times has the second time been better than the first for you? Not often. For most people, the most exciting time is the first time. That is the time you don't have a fixed point of view about it, so you have less projection and expectation of what it will be like. One night stands actually aren't that bad.

Most men have been taught that what makes sex exciting is the fact that it is forbidden. He is doing something he shouldn't do. Boys learn that as a little kid. "Touch that thing and I'll kill you." You are in the bathroom touching it as often as you can, but you have to get it over with fast because you could get caught. For most people, the sex that is forbidden is the valuable sex. When it is no longer forbidden (and the second time and the third time it is no longer forbidden), it becomes less valuable and it becomes less exciting, therefore most of the time it becomes less nurturing.

Are you saying, "No! It shouldn't be this way!" Okay, it shouldn't be this way. But is it this way? Yes, it is. For you to have a divorce-less relationship where you are having all of you, you have to see why relationship doesn't work, not how relationship ought to work. We all tend to look at how it ought to work rather than seeing how it actually works.

For men, the first time for the most part is considered the most exciting time because it is something new and strange. They are thinking, "What can I get away with? What can I do that is not considered correct?" Most human men want a new person every time. Humanoids like romance and cuddling and nurturing but they also want to have sex every time. Having no sex for a human-oid man is like, "What did I do wrong? What's wrong with me? Doesn't she love me? Why doesn't she care for me? Why is she not choosing me?" It may have nothing at all to do with you, but as a humanoid man, you will think it does.

This is how men have been trained and programmed. It is how sex has been set up in this reality. Does it have to be that way? No. Dain and I would like to encourage a different possibility, but we can't do that until you are willing to look at what is. Only then we can begin to show you a different possibility.

Sex Is Bad, Sex Is Good

Copulation is a judgeable offense. Having it is judgeable and not having it is judgeable. If you're having a lot of sex, you're a slut. If you're not having a lot of sex, you're stupid. For women, very often, sex is an audition for relationship. If you're a woman and you go out and have lots of sex, you're considered a bad girl. If you're a man and you go out and have lots of sex, you're considered a good stud. We aren't honest with ourselves about what copulation is to us.

The honesty of copulation would be like the animals, who do it just because it's time. They don't think it's wrong or right. It's just part of what you do. If we could be honest about copulation, then it could be like playing Frisbee. We make copulation meaningful. What if it meant nothing?

The honesty of copulation is to be able to ask, **"Will copulation improve what we already have?"** When you have copulation with someone, then everyone wants to know when you are getting married. They want to know what the next step is. Is a next step a reality? What's wrong with what you've got? When you eat the cookie on your plate, do you have a next step with that?

Does your family ask you who you are going out with and if you're getting married? Do you want to know how you get them to never ask you about it again? Say, "Yes, Mom, I have the best relationship I've ever had. I'm with two guys (girls) and I'm having sex with both of them at the same time and it's the best thing I've ever experienced." She will never ask you what's going on in your life again

The 1-2-3 Rule

The 1-2-3 rule applies to everybody, both men and women. The first time you have sex it is for fun, the second time you are in relationship, the third time you are getting married.

So you have got to be aware of what you want before you go there.

Exclusive Relationships

If you are creating a relationship with someone, how exclusive do you have to have it? The problem is that when you have an exclusive relationship, the first person you exclude from the relationship is you. If you are doing exclusive of any kind, you are doing separation. You are trying to separate this person from all others as though that creates them as just being with you. It doesn't really work. Separation is actually a lie. As an infinite being you are connected to everyone and everything, so you can't actually be separate. You can only cut off your awareness of your connection.

Why would you cut yourself off from everything else to be with one person? That seems to be the requirement of most relationships in contextual reality. What other choice do you have here? If you start with communion with yourself, you can add somebody to your life. If you don't have communion with you, then you will be looking for somebody else to fulfill you or to complete you. No one else can complete you; only you can complete you.

People with great relationships don't do exclusion. That means that they don't have to have the other person exclusively to themselves. It doesn't mean they go out and copulate with others, because they have way more fun with each other than they do with anybody else. It means they can each have a life separate from the other as an element of their relationship. They don't feel they have to do everything together; they actually have a life where they come together through choice, which makes the relationship a lot more fun.

Chapter Twenty-Seven

WHAT IS YOUR RELATIONSHIP
WITH MONEY?

Do you believe having more money will give you freedom? We make "freedom" our target and our goal, but choice is the source of being and receiving. To have the point of view that freedom is going to give you something, you have to first come to the judgment and conclusion that you have no freedom.

People say that if they had money they would have the freedom to choose anything. The reality is you already have the freedom to choose anything—but what do you choose? You choose things that require money, you choose things you think you can't have and you create your life based on that. Money is not the source of life.

Have you ever heard someone say, "If I had enough money I could be myself?" What? The truth is if you would be you, chances are the money would actually show up. Do you put money on a pedestal and worship it as if it is something that will come to you eventually because you're worshiping it? Do you believe that some day your ship will come in? The trouble is that "some day" is about how something is going to happen in the future and you never get to the future because every day is today.

Do you say, "I'm comfortable where I am and if I had more money than I currently have, I wouldn't know what to do with it?" How about asking, "What would it take for me to learn to do something with all this money?" It's just a choice.

Do you love money? Do you love having money and spending money? If you are not willing to acknowledge that you love money, how much of it are you going to be willing to have? How much of it can you have with ease?

Do you want to hang out with people who hate you, who won't acknowledge you and won't tell you that they are grateful for you? Not so much, right? Wouldn't you rather hang out with someone who loves you and isn't worried about letting other people know it? Well, it is the same thing with money. If you are willing to actually love it, acknowledge it and enjoy having it, it will flow to you.

Tool: If I Buy You, Will You Make Me Money?

Every molecule in the universe has consciousness, so with everything you buy, ask, **"If I buy you will you make me money?"** You are asking the molecular structure of that thing whether it will contribute to you and make your life expand. First of all, you do not own anything. Your furniture doesn't dust you; you dust it. Your car doesn't go to work to take care of you; you go to work

251

to take care of it. Everything outside of us doesn't belong to us; we belong to everything. It owns us. It contributes an energy that makes our life better. It expands our life. Therefore if we ask it to contribute to us, it will—and in very strange or surprising ways.

Also ask, **"Is it rewarding to buy this?"** Yes or no? This doesn't mean you should buy it because you are going to sell it for more money. It is not linear or logical; it is energetic. The energy of the thing creates a lightness, a sense that there's something more. That is the rewarding part.

People divorce a lot of themselves in order to spend money rather than to have money. You divorce a whole lot of you to not have too much money. You divorce huge amounts of you to make sure you have a money problem. What percentage of you do you have to divorce in order to have a money problem? Would you like us to tell you? Nine hundred ninety percent of you!

Self Debting

What if your point of view about money is something you bought from somebody else? What if it has nothing to do with you? You need to become aware of what you're doing with money. In our money classes, we recommend a book called *How to Get Out of Debt, Stay Out of Debt and Live Prosperously* by Jerrold Mundis. This book talks about people who go into debt and spend money they don't have. It begins to teach you how to be aware of how you spend money, how you waste money, how you function with money, and what's really important to you. It also talks about people who always put themselves last.

People who put themselves last are self-debtors, which means they value themselves not at all. This is not a good idea. Self-debtors believe that it is good to do things for others rather than themselves. They prefer contributing to everybody else's life rather than having one.

If you are one of those people who put everybody else's needs, wants and desires ahead of your own, you are a self-debtor of magnitude. You have no value to you. How is that working for you?

What Are You Working For?

Do you realize that in human reality (contextual reality) the purpose of life is death? That's the only purpose in life. What if you had a different purpose?

Have you spent your life trying to find your true purpose, your real purpose or your higher calling? Has it worked? What if the purpose of your life was to have fun? Are you having any yet?

Please give up having a hard life. We are taught from early on that if something is difficult to get, it must be valuable. What if the one thing that would make you the greatest amount of money in life was the thing you did most easily?

Do what you are good at. Doing what you are good at will create what you are asking for. Don't try to be something you are not. People come to conclusions about what is going to create others doing things with them, but what works is being fantastic in what you are fantastic at.

There is an idea in this reality that work is something you do that you don't really want to do. What if what you did as work was something you enjoyed? What if the thing that generated money for you was something you enjoyed? What if it was fun for you?

The To Do List

Do you make a To Do list each day? Do you begin by accomplishing a lot of things, but then you start adding as many things to the list as you have accomplished? If you give that up and say, "Oh well, I will accomplish whatever I get accomplished" you will find you accomplish ten times as much.

All the list does is fixate you on what you think you have to do so you don't have any real choice. Get rid of your To Do list and function from the questions: "What do I need to do today? What's really important today? What do I have to accomplish?" Don't function from a list, function from your awareness of what has to be accomplished.

When you are willing to be aware, that which needs to be handled will yell at you and you will get it done. Just ask, "Where do I have to put my energy and attention today?"

There are tons of things on your To Do list that it is not yet time for you to do, so it's not going to work. If you wait until the task is ready to be done, it will tell you. It will come into your awareness and you will know that today is the day to pay attention to it—and you'll do it.

Lack of Motivation

When you choose to function from above the 10%, you will step into the energy that generates everything and you will lose what you think is the energy you need to create from. It will feel like you have lost the impetus and motivation of your life because the motivation is based on the contraction of the 10%. When you move into the 990%, suddenly you have a different possibility. When you are doing things from the 10%, it feels intense. You feel like you are creating something. As soon as the energy moves into a greater realm where you start to be successful, you move into space. When that occurs, the intense energy is gone and you may assume you have lost the impetus for what you are working on. You don't realize that the energy must move into space so what you are creating can grow and become something greater.

Oftentimes when you move from the 10% to the 12%, you stop contributing, you stop generating and you stop giving energy to whatever you are creating because it doesn't have the solidity of the 10%. The moment you feel light, you assume that nothing is happening and you pull your energy out of what's going to expand your life. You can't feel that familiar density anymore so you assume whatever you've been creating is going away. You think it's not going to come into existence or fruition. This is one of the reasons why many people do start-stop, start-stop, start-stop rather than create in a continuous forward movement.

Please recognize that when anything becomes light, it has become a life form of its own. This occurs with everything that we create. For example, if you are creating a new business, at a certain point it begins to grow of its own volition because it now has an energy that attracts people who desire it. When that happens, you may tend to think you are not putting enough energy into it. If it doesn't feel like the contractive 10%, you think you are not applying enough to it to keep it going.

At that point you say, "Everything is going away. It's going to fail!" Ninety-nine percent of all failures occur when you get to 11% because you go out of solidity into the possibilities of the non-contextual universe. Generation occurs above 10% so anything above 10% will generate an ongoing possibility.

The trick is to just keep the energy there and realize that whatever you're creating is now turning into the space where it can be whatever it is that you created it as. The project itself is actually now willing to have a consciousness of its own. It is willing to contribute to you, so just keep putting energy there and ask it what the next step is. We tend to pull our energy out because we think nothing is working, but you will go forward faster and larger if you're willing to keep your energy in it. Ask, "What can I contribute now that will make this thing become hugely successful?"

What creates the most money? Perspiration or inspiration? Inspiration. When you are doing the 10% you're doing perspiration, and the moment you move into the 12% or greater you are moving into inspiration. That is the moment in which great money can come to you, so don't quit!

You have a choice in life, you can be creative or you can be generative. If you are generative, your life is like a battery that just keeps putting out juice. If you are creative, you have to destroy something in order to create something, and the first thing you tend to destroy in order to create something new is some part of you. You will even destroy your body with drugs and alcohol in order to create something new in your life.

What if you didn't have to destroy anything to create your life? What if your life was a constant state of generation?

Chapter Twenty-Eight

GENERATING A DIFFERENT REALITY FOR YOUR LIFE

There is a point of view out there that there should be a balance of happiness and sadness in a person's life. The idea is you will experience as much happiness as sadness, and you need to have a balance between the two. Does that feel light to you? No. The truth is that the majority of life can be lived in happiness and joy. There doesn't have to be a positive and negative charge for everything. What if there was just generative energy?

In order to have a positive and negative point of view, you have to have a judgment. So for there to be happiness or sadness you have to have a judgment about what it is. Generative energy does not require judgment, and therefore it doesn't have a positive or negative point of view. There does not have to be balance in anything; there's just choice.

Generating Your Own Reality

When you have your own reality, you do everything differently because you only do what works for you. Things happen differently for you than they do for other people because you are willing to generate your life from question, choice, possibilities and contribution. What if you could generate your whole life from just asking for it to show up?

Have you ever had an experience of something that goes missing and you look for it and you look for it and you look for it, and then it shows up in some crazy place? There is no way in hell you would have put it there. You say, "That is so weird. I don't remember putting that there." But if you didn't put it there, then that is not where you put it. You had to create it there or take it from one place and put it in another place without using your hand. So how about saying, "Wow, I can generate anything I choose to generate if I am willing to generate it."

A lady told us the story of how she generated her reality with the question she was asking about her relationship. One day while she was wondering if she had a good relationship, she opened her mail. The first letter she opened was from Access Consciousness. It was advertising the Divorceless Relationship Class. She read it and said, "That is exactly what I am looking for." Then she saw the price and asked, "Okay, how am I going to get this?" She opened up the next letter, which was a tax return, and there was the price of the class.

This is the way you start to generate your life: question, choice, possibilities and contribution.

Tool: The Power Ball Exercise

If you are not happy with your life, if you are not getting what you want financially, if you don't have any idea what you want to do but you just know you need to change the way you are living, this exercise can help you get clear about what you would like to create as your life.

How do you create the partner you want, the life you want, the job you want or whatever it is you are looking for? In order to get anything you desire in life, you have to first be aware of what it is you desire.

Creating Your Power Ball

Step 1: *Ask, "What would I like my life to look like and be like?" Get the energy of that and put it in a ball out in front of you.*

Step 2: *Pull energy into it from all over the universe and let little trickles go out to all those people who are looking for you and don't know it.*

Step 3: *Anything that shows up in your life that feels like the energy you described in step 1, whether it makes sense to you or not, go do it. Follow that energy.*

Step 1: Get Clear About What You Would Like to Have as Your Life

This doesn't have to be a big list but it does have to have space in it for infinite possibilities. Don't limit it by being too specific. For example, the elements I wanted in my life were to have a job where I traveled at least two weeks out of every month, to never get bored, to always do something that expanded people's lives in a way that was joyful and fun for me, and to generate at least $100,000 a year. That was the whole list.

If you would like to have a relationship, ask, "What would I like my relationship to look like?" Be clear about it and get the way it would feel to have it in your life. When you pull energy into it, you are actually pulling in the person and the circumstance that will allow that relationship to show up.

If you write down "freedom to be me," be aware that freedom is a lie. You always have freedom to choose. It is a lie that you don't have freedom. To ask for freedom is asking for a limitation because you're trying to undo something you've already decided you don't have and doesn't exist.

Let's say you write down "infinite choice and fun" as the criteria you have for creating a relationship. How many of your relationships have been about fun and choice? None. Why? Because you have not been clear about what you would really like to have as a relationship.

Then do you beat yourself up because you don't know what you want? Do you realize you have created relationship as a torture, not as a possibility? Do you get that most of your relationships have been torture for you? Even though you think you know what you want, you have no idea what you want—so what you get instead is the torture, the shame, the blame, the regret and the judgment.

Oftentimes you end up with torturous relationships because you don't truly desire a relationship—but you think we are supposed to desire one. Because you have no clarity about what you would like to have as a relationship, you go around making sure you don't have a relationship, that's the torture part; "How can I make sure I don't have a relationship while claiming I wish to have a relationship?"

When you make the demand to get clear about what you would like as your relationship, then you can ask for it. You can't ask until you're aware about it.

Some people want things that are very specific: "I want a green BMW parked in the garage of my seven bedroom house in Noosa, Australia." What if you want something that is not specific? What if what you want is an energy? When you get the energy of what you would like your life to be like, it's not a feeling; it is an awareness of the energy and how it permeates your body, your life and your universe. To get a sense of it you can ask, "What would I like my life to feel like?" but it is not actually a feeling because your life is an energy. When you look at what you would really like to have, is it the thing itself—or is it the energy? It's the energy of it, right?

Be willing to recognize what *you* would like to have in your life and figure out what it is for yourself. Don't choose someone else's idea or it will backfire on you big time.

Step 2: Pull Energy

Get all the elements of what you would like to have as your relationship and get the energy of that. Once you have an awareness of the energy of what you would like your life to be, put it in a ball out in front of you and pull energy into it from all over the whole universe. The universe is a very large place. Pull energy into your energy ball until your heart opens up—then let little trickles go out to everyone and everything that's going to help you make it a reality. Let little trickles go out to all the people you are looking for that are looking for you and don't know it yet.

When somebody shows up, acknowledge that you are getting what you asked for. That's the important part. Keep pulling the energy into it until you get what you're looking for.

Step 3: Keep Asking Questions

Pull this energy in and when someone shows up, stay in the question. Don't go to conclusion. When you say, "that means x, y, z," you are going into the significance of something. Having someone show up doesn't mean anything except that now you can have something you always thought you wanted. Now that you have it, do you really want it? Now that you have it, what do you do with it?

If someone shows up and they are the same sex, recognize that you are getting what you asked for. It doesn't mean you have to copulate with them, it doesn't mean you have to create a relationship with them, but you could create a friendship with them if you choose. So maybe the same sex shows up, maybe the other sex shows up; it doesn't matter because you can continue to ask for more.

Doing this exercise doesn't mean you have to choose the first person who comes along. Most people make the mistake of saying, "Oh, at last!" Is that a question? It is not a question. So, when someone shows up ask, "Is this the person I want to spend my life with? What period of time could I spend with this person?" For most humanoids, anything over five years is a serious long-term commitment.

Remember, for you as a humanoid there are a lot of places in your life where the only way you find out what you want is to find out what you don't want. It could be that you thought you wanted this person or this relationship your whole life. Now that it has shown up and you have the chance to experience it, do you truly wish to have it or desire it? And for how long do you desire this?

Question leads to awareness.

Make a Demand

If you want something to happen, you have to make a demand, not just pull energy into it from all over the universe. You must make a demand of yourself.

What do I have to be, do, have, create or generate that would allow this to come to fruition? *Everything that doesn't allow that to show up times a godzillion, I destroy and uncreate it all. Right and wrong, good and bad, POD and POC, all nine, shorts, boys and beyonds.*

Then whatever shows up, do It.

The power ball is about generating your life. Ask, "What would I like to have in my life? I would like to have a relationship, I'd like a business, and I'd like to have a bigger life. So what would a bigger life look like to me? I'd like it to feel like this...." It is not a desire; it is what you would like to generate as your life.

Look through your life like an old photo album and ask, "What part of my life was really fun? When was I enjoying every moment of it?" Those were the moments when you were choosing your reality, not someone else's. "When did I enjoy being alone?" That was choosing your own reality. Those are the moments from which you can identify what the basis of your reality can be. You have to be willing to look at that, choose that, and ask, "What else would I like to have as my reality?" You have always chosen your reality based on somebody else's needs, wants, and desires, not yours. This is a beginning. It requires you to actually choose and work it out.

What Is Generative Energy?

Generative energy is a level of presence and awareness that has to do with the energy that generates something. It is not the energy that creates something. When you put a lot of effort and energy into something, that's creative energy. Generative energy occurs when you look at something and a door begins to open. Let's say you decided you were interested in macadamia nuts, and you ask, "I wonder what it would take to have macadamia nuts in my life?" Then you turn a corner and there's somebody with a tree saying, "Anybody want my macadamia nut tree? I'm getting rid of this thing." Things happen quickly and easily when you're doing generative energy. But when you're putting a lot of energy and effort into something, you're using the force of creation and construction, and it takes much longer to bring something into existence.

Do you have a point of view about how long something should take? You are judging the time something takes rather than asking, "How can this happen more quickly in the future?" or "How can I generate this?" You assume that what you are asking for should happen instantaneously every time, but you can't make things happen that are not ready to happen. Be willing for something to show up when it shows up.

Everything has a life form of its own. You are the source for generating the energy that allows the energy ball to function, but when it begins to have a life form of its own, you tend to stop drawing energy into it. Most of us either think we have to continue to create or that we don't have to do anything once something takes off on its own. No, you still have to contribute. It's like having a child; you have to give them a certain amount of energy and you have to receive a certain amount of energy from them. One day they start generating their own life but you still have to contribute to them until the day you die.

Chapter Twenty-Nine

MOVING ABOVE THE
10 PERCENT IN RELATIONSHIP

If you are contracting yourself to the 10% so you can feel human, when you start to create something, you create within that 10% model. It feels dense and intense, like there is a lot going on, and then just at the moment when success is about to occur, it moves into the 12% to 15% category and it becomes very light. How does this work in relationship?

Your relationship starts with attraction and lust. It's that "I love this person so intensely" feeling, and then it goes to a generative energy, which feels lighter, and you think the relationship is failing. So you try to create intensity with the person in order to know you are back in the 10%. This causes problems every time. You start creating trauma and drama, upset and intrigue because that means you are in the intensity again.

When a relationship moves into the energy above the 10%, there is a sense of peace, a sense of relaxation and a sense of possibility, but people assume that if it moves there they are not going to have the intense sex and love anymore. They assume the honeymoon is over. No, from this space, you can have something that is more expansive for both of you.

A great many of us learned this way of creating when we were kids. We have parents who have to do some form of trauma and drama as soon as everything is going okay. Our parents live according to the 10% and once life gets beyond that, they say, "Oh well, that can't happen. It can't be that easy. What's the catch? Something is wrong!" You have learned that the intensity, which is the same thing you think you are getting when you first find someone, is what relationship is supposed to be.

What we are presenting in this book is a completely different possibility. It is something that moves beyond the 10% intensity of relationship and into the 990%. What would be possible for you in relationship if you knew to look for the peace and possibility of the 990% as something you actually desired?

Relationship at 990%

The whole world functions from this kind of intense relationship at the moment. You might ask, "How do I deal with it and choose something else?" You don't have to deal with it. When you are functioning in 990% of possibility, the intensity is just an awareness that you have. Whenever you go above the 10%, you can have an awareness of a different choice. You can say, "Wow, that is really intense. Do I want to be with this person? No thanks. See you later. Adios. Goodbye."

With the awareness of the 990% available in relationship, you can ask for another possibility. When you meet someone, ask energetically, "Okay, do they have the capacity to do the 990%?" Trust your knowing. If you know they have the capacity or the willingness, you can ask, "Would they be willing to go here? Would they be willing to go on the adventure of finding out what this could be like?" If they are, you have the capacity to create something phenomenal that has never existed before. If they are not, you can say to yourself, "You are really cute, I'd love to have sex with you, and I am not going to do that right now because I am not willing to dive into the 10% cesspool. Thank you very much, bye-bye!"

The world functions from the 10%. Does that mean you have to? No.

Communion

Are you aware that "doing relationship" is one of the major ways you cut off your awareness? What is the other possibility beyond relationship? Communion and oneness. If you and I are in relationship, by definition we are not oneness, right? So if you are functioning from the idea of relationship can you have the awareness you desire? No.

Communion is the inclusion of everything, the judgment of nothing and the willingness to receive everything just as it is with no point of view. When you have an awareness of this space of total receiving, it can bring up a welling of what feels like "emotion" in your body, your life and your being. It is actually an awareness of expansiveness rather than an emotion. Emotion is a contraction.

Some people learn about communion and they say, "Oh, I want a communion with someone." The thing is communion is something you have with *everything,* not with *someone.* "Communion with someone" means relationship, which is not what you desire. You have to be in communion with you and with the Earth and with everything around you, so there would be no separation between you and the chair you are sitting on. You would have communion with the chair, and if it wasn't soft enough you could ask, "Chair, can you make yourself comfortable enough that you don't hurt my body?" Try it!

If you are truly in communion with all things, then you are in the place of oneness, consciousness and communion with every molecule in the world. When you ask for the molecules to change and become something different, they do. You don't have the right of life or death, you can't make somebody die and you can't make somebody not die. But you do have the opportunity to change what's fixed in their universe that's affecting you in an adverse way.

Tool: All of Life Comes to Me with Ease and Joy and Glory

The mantra of Access Consciousness is **All of life comes to me with ease and joy and glory.** This is the best description of what communion is. Using this mantra will bring you to an awareness that you can function in life from ease and joy and glory no matter what occurs. Glory is an exuberant expression of abundance, and it ought to be a comfortable, joyous life right? This is about all of life...the good the bad, the beautiful and the ugly. Everything is included and nothing is judged.

All of life comes to me with ease and joy and glory is a mantra, it is not an affirmation. What has your experience been with affirmations? Do they work? When you are making affirmations, have you noticed that the opposite side of what you are affirming shows up? Why? Because as soon as you make the affirmation, you have decided the other side of it is where the power is. You are doing the affirmation in an attempt to overcome the power source. What if there was no power source other than you?

Saying the mantra **"All life comes to me of with ease, joy, and glory"** ten times in the morning and ten times at night will change your life because it is about the energy of communion. It invites the universe to assist you.

My oldest son had been to four drug programs with no good result. I had done everything that "could be done" in this reality; I had even called prayer lines. Nothing had worked. One night he went out in my car and he was gone. Hours passed. Not knowing what else to do, I kept saying, **"All of life comes to me with ease and joy and glory."** I kept saying it until I fell asleep and every time I woke up, I would start saying it again, because my son was not yet home.

At 7:30 in the morning he finally walked in the house. I said, "Okay, what's the deal?" Something had definitely changed, because my son said, "I need a drug program. I have to go away someplace where I'll be locked up for a long period of time to get over this."

Chapter Thirty

LIFE AS ADVENTURE

What if your life could actually be an adventure? What if it weren't about "I've got to wake up again today and I've got to do this and I've got to do that?" What if you came out of obligation and into the adventure you could have as your life?

Do you realize that you refuse the adventure of your life and you insert humdrum boredom instead? You try to become like other people. Do you realize how much energy it takes when you to try to make yourself be like other people? You are killing your body when you try to squash you into the square peg or the round hole you're trying to get into.

You can try to change what is not working into something that will work or you can *do something entirely different.* You have already instituted your life as it is. Would you like something different or would you like to stick with what you've got? Don't try to fix your life or change it—choose something different.

When something doesn't work, say, "Well, that didn't work the way I wanted it to. What else is possible here?" When you start down a roadway and it turns into a dead end, do you stop driving and say, "I can't get there?" Or do you turn around and go back the way you came for a little while until you find another place to turn? Your life is never a completion; it is just a bunch of different turns you can make.

What if you invented your life every ten seconds instead of trying to invent your life from your past, from the future you think you should have, from the things that didn't work out in your life or from the things that you thought you got right? What if you just enjoyed this ten seconds totally, absolutely and irrevocably?

Would you be willing to go on the adventure of your life and discover just how much of you has been hiding all this time? Would you like to reclaim all the parts and pieces of you that you have divorced so you can fit in this 10% reality? You can always go back to the cesspool if you don't like the clear pool. We don't mind what you choose so long as you know you have choice. The 990% is there for you to choose anytime you are ready.

Glossary

Bars

The bars are a hands-on Access process that involves a light touch upon the head to contact points that correspond to different aspects of one's life. There are points for joy, sadness, body and sexuality, awareness, kindness, gratitude, peace and calm. There is even a money bar. These points are called bars because they run from one side of the head to the other.

Be

In this book, the word *be* is sometimes used to refer to you, the infinite being you truly be, as opposed to a contrived point of view about who you think you are.

Clearing Statement (POD/POC)

The clearing statement we use in Access is: Right and wrong, good and bad, POD, POC, all nine, shorts, boys and beyonds.

Right and wrong, good and bad is shorthand for: What's good, perfect and correct about this? What's wrong, mean, vicious, terrible, bad and awful about this? What's right and wrong, good and bad?

POC is the point of creation of the thoughts, feelings and emotions immediately preceding whatever you decided.

POD is the point of destruction immediately preceding whatever you decided. It's like pulling the bottom card out of a house of cards. The whole thing falls down.

All nine stands for nine layers of crap that were taken out. You know that somewhere in those nine layers, there's got to be a pony because you couldn't put that much shit in one place without having a pony in there. It's shit that you're generating yourself, which is the bad part.

Shorts is the short version of: What's meaningful about this? What's meaningless about this? What's the punishment for this? What's the reward for this?

Boys stands for nucleated spheres. Have you ever seen one of those kids' bubble pipes? Blow here and you create a mass of bubbles. You pop one bubble and the other bubbles fill in the space.

Beyonds are feelings or sensations you get that stop your heart, stop your breath, or stop your willingness to look at possibilities. It's like when your business is in the red and you get another final notice and you say *argh!* You weren't expecting that right now.

Sometimes, instead of saying "use the clearing statement," we just say, "POD and POC it."

About Gary M. Douglas

20 years ago, Gary M. Douglas started to develop Access Consciousness with the knowing that a different way of functioning in the world must be possible. His purpose with Access is to create a world of consciousness and oneness—where consciousness includes everything and judges nothing.

Simple, effective, and to the point, Access is a set of tools, processes and questions that enable people to create change in any area of their life.

Born in the American Midwest and raised in San Diego, California, Mr. Douglas as always been on a spiritual path, seeking deeper answers to life's mysteries. His innate curiosity has allowed him to question what didn't seem to be working in life and to seek alternatives to the popular views and accepted wisdom of today. He has been married twice and has four children.

Today Mr. Douglas' workshops can be found in 25 countries and is offered by over 600 facilitators worldwide. Mr. Douglas continues to travel all over the world facilitating advanced classes on subjects ranging from bodies, the Earth, animals, conscious children, possibilities, relationship and money.

The techniques of Access Consciousness are being used world-wide to transform lives and bodies in private practices as well as in conjunction with addiction recovery, weight loss, business and money, animal health and many holistic health modalities, such as acupuncture and chiroporactic care. Mr. Douglas has written several books on the subjects of money, sex, relationship, magic and animals. In 2010, "The Place" became a Barnes and Nobel bestseller.

To find out more, visit

www.GaryMDouglas.com

www.accessconsciousness.com

www.isnowthetime.com

www.accesstheplace.com

About Dr. Dain Heer

Dr. Dain Heer travels all over the world facilitating advanced classes on Access Consciousness. He invites and inspires people to more consciousness from total allowance, caring, humor and a phenomenal knowing.

Within Access, Dr. Heer has developed a unique energy process for change for individuals and groups, called The Energetic Synthesis of Being. Dr. Dain Heer has a completely different approach to change. He teaches people to tap into and recognize their own abilities and knowing. The energetic transformation possible is fast—and truly dynamic.

Dr. Heer started work as a Network Chiropractor eleven years ago in California. Having worked with bodies since he was in college, Dr. Heer came across Access Consciousness at a point in his life when he was deeply unhappy and even planning suicide.

Access Consciousness changed everything. When none of the other modalities and techniques Dr. Heer had been studying were giving him lasting results or change, with Access Consciousness, his life began to expand and grow with more ease and speed than even he could have imagined possible.

Dr. Heer has written a series of books on the topics of embodiment, healing, money and relationships.

To find out more, visit

www.DrDainHeer.com

www.accessconsciousness.com

Other Access Consciousness Books

The Place
2010 Barnes and Noble #1 Best-Selling Novel. "In this book you may find out what you have always been looking for, and how and where it may exist."

Talk to the Animals
Did you know that every animal, every plant, every structure on this planet has consciousness and desires to gift to you?

Money Isn't the Problem, You Are
Offering out-of-the box concepts with money. It's not about money. It never is. It's about what you're willing to receive.

Sex Is Not a Four Letter Word, but Relationship Often Times Is
Funny, frank and delightfully irreverent, this book offers readers an entirely fresh view of how to create great intimacy and exceptional sex.

Magic. You Are It. Be It.
Magic is about the fun of having the things you desire. The real magic is the ability to have the joy that life can be.

Right Riches for You!
What if money could work for you instead of you working for money? Tools to empower you to change your financial situation with ease and permanence. As seen on Lifetime Television's *Balancing Act Show.*

www.accessconsciousness.com

CPSIA information can be obtained at www.ICGtesting.com
Printed in the USA
LVOW010921310513

336298LV00009B/310/P